The Area of Freedom, Security and Justice ten years on

Successes and future challenges under the Stockholm Programme

THE AREA OF FREEDOM, SECURITY AND JUSTICE TEN YEARS ON

SUCCESSES AND FUTURE CHALLENGES UNDER THE STOCKHOLM PROGRAMME

EDITORS
ELSPETH GUILD
SERGIO CARRERA
AND
ALEJANDRO EGGENSCHWILER

CENTRE FOR EUROPEAN POLICY STUDIES
BRUSSELS

The Centre for European Policy Studies (CEPS) is an independent policy research institute based in Brussels. Its mission is to produce sound analytical research leading to constructive solutions to the challenges facing Europe today.

This paperback is published in the context of IN:EX, a three-year project on converging and conflicting ethical values in the internal/external security continuum in Europe, funded by the Security Programme of DG Enterprise of the European Commission's 7th Framework Research Programme.

The opinions expressed in this publication and the analysis and arguments given are the sole responsibility of the authors writing in a personal capacity and do not necessarily reflect those of CEPS or any other institution with which the authors are associated.

ISBN 978-94-6138-034-0

Centre for European Policy Studies
Place du Congrès 1, B-1000 Brussels
Tel: 32 (0) 2 229.39.11 Fax: 32 (0) 2 219.41.51
e-mail: info@ceps.eu
internet: http://www.ceps.eu

Contents

1. THE EUROPEAN UNION'S AREA OF FREEDOM, SECURITY AND JUSTICE TEN YEARS ON

ELSPETH GUILD AND SERGIO CARRERA

Introduction

In 1999, the Amsterdam Treaty formally created the European Union's Area of Freedom, Security and Justice (AFSJ), which includes policing, judicial cooperation in criminal and civil matters, border controls, immigration, asylum and related fields that normally fall under the interior, justice and home affairs ministries of member states. Since then, the AFSJ has become one of the key political priorities for the European Union. Ten years have passed and the main institutional, policy, legal and financial foundations of this AFSJ have largely been established. During this time, the promulgation of AFSJ EU law and policy has been sensitive to events and political dynamics at the international, European and national levels. This has gone hand in hand with continuing hesitations in certain EU member states as to the added value of having 'more Europe' in fields traditionally and deeply rooted in national sovereignty and the principle of subsidiarity. The intergovernmental approach has been much in evidence in the AFSJ but has not prevented Europeanisation from moving forward, something that has come as a surprise to both internal and external observers. Policies as diverse as border controls, immigration, asylum, European citizenship and freedom of movement, cooperation in criminal justice and police now have clear EU dimensions with profound implications (and challenges) not only for member states' competences, but also for the liberty and security of individuals and the principles upon which the EU is founded. Among the most important issues for European cooperation on AFSJ during these last ten years has been how to ensure that these European norms and decision-making structures are fully compatible with liberal democratic principles of accountability, the rule of law and fundamental rights. This will remain one of the main topics to address in the next phase of the AFSJ.

The Treaty of Lisbon and the Stockholm Programme of December 2009 aim at overcoming some of the dilemmas of the AFSJ by offering a renewed institutional and policy framework upon which the next generation of AFSJ measures will be built. The Lisbon Treaty does away with the 'first pillar/third pillar divide' and makes the EU Charter of Fundamental Rights legally binding. These changes will revolutionise the way in which the AFSJ works and the paths it is expected to take from now on. The third multiannual programme on AFSJ policies endorsed by the European Council – the Stockholm Programme – has additionally set an ambitious agenda for the next five years in which *the kinds* of common policies that are being developed and the evaluation of their *implementation* and *effects* on fundamental human rights and the rule of law principles have moved to centre stage. Now a critical aspect concerns how these foundations and priorities are transformed into norms and practices in the AFSJ.

The tenth anniversary of the AFJS and its renewed political and legal elements provide us with a unique opportunity to reflect on the successes and challenges of the last ten years of European cooperation on these important policies. The Justice and Home Affairs (JHA) Section of the Centre for European Policy Studies has been actively engaged in providing independent (policy-relevant) research assessing the major policy developments that have taken place during this timeframe. (See the list of publications in Appendix I of this volume.) The JHA Section has also played a role in channelling interdisciplinary academic findings and debates around these topics to policy-making processes at the European level and to the work of the main European institutions. We consider the occasion of the AFSJ's tenth birthday an appropriate moment to solicit the views of a selected group of policy-makers and practitioners who have been and continue to be influential in the thinking about the contours of the EU's AFSJ. This books aims at celebrating the AFSJ's birthday by bringing together their first-hand accounts of the major achievements so far and the dilemmas ahead for the next generation of the EU's AFSJ.

This book reflects upon the experiences of the first phase of the EU's AFSJ (1999–2009), as well as on possible ways forward in the building of its next phase. The first six chapters cover several horizontal aspects related to the new policy and Treaty-based framework emerging from the Treaty of Lisbon and the Stockholm Programme. These are then complemented by a set of contributions focusing on some of the most important achievements and difficulties in specific AFSJ policy domains, in particular those related to asylum, border controls, and judicial cooperation in criminal matters and police. This first chapter aims at setting the scene and introducing some of the main issues and findings of the contributions making up this collective volume.

A renewed policy and treaty-based architecture for the AFSJ: The Lisbon Treaty and the Stockholm Programme

The political and executive architecture of the AFSJ has been a matter of substantial institutional restlessness since the early 1990s. From the Maastricht Treaty (which first formally acknowledged the existence of a JHA dimension to the EU) to the Lisbon Treaty (which has given an EU constitutional dimension to the field), almost 20 years have passed. The road has not been smooth; there have been many false steps along the way. The end of 2009 gave the AFSJ a new institutional, decision making and legal shape. The entry into force of the Lisbon Treaty has marked a 'before and after' point in the making of the EU's AFSJ. The new configurations contained in the Treaty on the Functioning of the European Union and the revised version of the Treaty on European Union provide an excellent basis for ambitious ways forward in European policy-making in these domains.

One of the main deficits that has characterised EU cooperation on AFSJ during the last ten years has been the first/third pillar divide, which presented a loose institutional structure favouring intergovernmental approaches that often resulted in less than clear legal outputs, especially concerning police and judicial cooperation in criminal matters. Moreover, the previous Treaty framework allowed for the non-applicability of the ordinary legislative procedure (the former co-decision procedure) to policy areas such as regular immigration (conditions for entry and residence) and the integration of non-EU nationals, and limited the jurisdiction of the Court of Justice in Luxembourg when interpreting and reviewing adopted legal acts. All this has gone alongside a vulnerable setting for the protection of the fundamental rights of individuals. The Treaty of Lisbon has put a 'formal' end to some of these vulnerabilities through the abolition of the pillar structure (the expansion of the European method of cooperation). It has also provided new legal bases for enacting far-reaching European legislation, widened the competences of the Court of Justice and converted the EU Charter of Fundamental Rights into a legally binding bill of rights for Europe.

The institutional elements of the EU's AFSJ have been regularly accompanied by strategies for setting the policy agenda. Since 1999, the European Council has adopted five-year political programmes outlining the EU's agenda driving AFSJ policies and the timetables for their accomplishment. The first one was the Tampere Programme (October 1999), adopted under the Finnish presidency, which endorsed a very ambitious plan corresponding with the high expectations about the possibilities offered by the Amsterdam Treaty. Along with the barriers encountered by the European Commission when translating the political ambitions into actual legal outputs, and as the contribution by Karl von Wogau outlines, the events of 11 September 2001 and 11 March 2004 provoked a prioritisation of certain (internal and external) security initiatives (chiefly enshrined in the European security strategy). These focused on the so-called 'fight against terrorism', which in many respects overtook those falling under the umbrella of freedom and justice.

The prevalence of the security rationale was directly reflected in the nature and priorities structuring the second-multiannual programme on an AFSJ – The Hague Programme (November 2004) adopted by the Dutch presidency. The Hague programme gave preference to the security of the Union and its member states, and understood the EU's AFSJ as primarily driven by security (urgency-led) considerations and concerns. The Hague Programme also invented the metaphor of a 'balance' between freedom and security, calling for the need to strike the right balance between law enforcement purposes and safeguarding the fundamental rights of individuals. Overall, the political elements of the EU's AFSJ agenda have been vulnerable to political demands for more 'security cooperation' within and outside Europe, perhaps without paying due consideration to the effects on and ethical implications of these very security policies for the liberal democratic principles, fundamental rights and liberties at the heart of the EU.

In contrast with its predecessor, the Stockholm Programme – the third multiannual programme adopted by the Swedish presidency (December 2009) – no longer speaks of a 'balance' to be struck between liberty and security. As the contribution by Jacques Barrot demonstrates, it has rather placed a "Europe of rights" as the premise upon which any security measures need to be founded. As Barrot argues, the Stockholm Programme is the EU's response to open questions about the ways in which people's rights are respected (and empowered) and their security protected. Indeed, the Stockholm Programme departs from its predecessor (The Hague Programme) by stating that "[t]he challenge will be to ensure respect for fundamental freedoms and integrity while guaranteeing security in Europe. It is of paramount importance that law enforcement measures and measures to safeguard individual rights, the rule of law, [and] international protection rules go hand in hand in the same direction and are mutually reinforced."[1]

In light of the above, the two critical dilemmas for the future generation of the AFSJ are the following: First, how and to what extent will these new Treaty-based and policy elements be translated into practical and effective outputs? Second, how are the various interests and roles of the different actors going to be balanced under the new decision-making and institutional arrangements?

The first immediate, visible result has been changes within the European Commission and the directorate-general responsible for AFSJ policies (the Directorate-General for Justice, Freedom and Security, DG JLS). One of the key proponents of a clearly formulated and specific set of powers for JHA in this field has been Berlin's Senate Department for Justice, which has advocated an independent justice portfolio since 2007. As Hasso Lieber's contribution highlights, this division is actually a European standard and "the balancing of interests by means of reciprocal control is part of the separation of powers that already exists in all of the member states". As the AFSJ enters its second decade, it has finally achieved this. The Commission's DG JLS is being divided into two parts – Commissioner Viviane Reding is taking charge of the justice portfolio (more specifically, justice, fundamental rights and citizenship) and Commissioner Cecilia Malmström the home affairs one. This separation is critical to ensuring coherence between EU and member state governance structures and the effective implementation of regulations in both spheres.

---

[1] See Council of the European Union, The Stockholm Programme – An open and secure Europe serving and protecting the citizens, 17024/09, Brussels, 2 December 2009.

It will also permit a clearer focus on the application and embedding of the EU Charter of Fundamental Rights in the core of both portfolios.

Another result, which has somewhat surprised certain external commentators and actors not only at the European Commission and Council, but also in non-EU countries such as the US, has been the effect of the enhanced position of the European Parliament as a co-legislator. The last ten years of European cooperation on AFSJ has taken place against a background of weak democratic accountability and scrutiny, where the European Parliament has too often been relegated to mere 'consultation' in areas having a deep impact on basic democratic principles and fundamental freedoms. A democratic deficit has also affected discussions on strategic agenda-setting, such as in the three multiannual programmes on an AFSJ (Tampere, The Hague and Stockholm), which have been exclusively in the hands of the European Council and with the exception of the Stockholm Programme have developed through non-transparent methods. As has been demonstrated by the European Parliament's rejection of the SWIFT agreement between the EU and the US because of its effects on privacy and data protection, things are rather different after the Treaty of Lisbon. Emilio De Capitani's chapter emphasises the importance of increasing democratic accountability for the EU's AFSJ and its agencies. Efficient cooperation between the European Parliament and national parliaments and the establishment of inter-parliamentary oversight will be crucial.

Various contributions to this volume have also highlighted the expanded role of national courts and the Court of Justice in Luxembourg as one of the most important innovations brought by the Lisbon Treaty, which will have major implications for the oversight and interpretation of EU AFSJ law. The growing judicialisation that is expected in areas such as immigration, asylum, criminal justice or police cooperation will indeed constitute a positive central component in ensuring a more consistent and accurate application of EU AFSJ law, and in guaranteeing the protection and respect of the individual's European freedoms and rights in all these policy domains.

The substantive elements of the AFSJ: Borders, asylum, criminal justice and police cooperation

The AFSJ is composed of a diverse and complex set of policy areas including, among others, issues related to judicial cooperation in criminal matters, police cooperation, immigration, asylum, borders and European citizenship. All of these areas have profound implications for the relationship between liberty and security in Europe, as well as for the fundamental rights of individuals. The compatibility of current and future proposals with the EU Charter of Fundamental Rights (hereafter the 'EU Charter') and the European Convention of Human Rights (ECHR) will therefore be another topic of paramount importance for the future. A selection of domains in which more 'progress' (in terms of the level of policy convergence) has been achieved during the last ten years is the focus of several contributions to this collective volume, which we now turn to synthesise.

Borders, privacy and data protection

The last 25 years of European cooperation on border controls have been very dynamic and these efforts are now covered by the Integrated Border Management (IBM) strategy. The Amsterdam Treaty transferred part of the Schengen *acquis* to European competence. Since then, the EU has managed to develop a common corpus of legislation (the Schengen Borders Code) and to set up an EU agency coordinating border-control surveillance operations (Frontex). The challenge for the future will be the development of better strategies for ensuring the rule of law and fundamental rights in the practical application of these substantive institutional instruments of the IBM. This goes along with discussions concerning the increasing use of technology in border management activities. The EU has favoured the use of technological tools and databases, such as the Schengen Information System (SIS) (and the ongoing development of its second generation (SIS II) and the Visa Information System) and the new proposals envisaged by the European Commission's 2008 border package, which have been subject to various concerns from different directions. As Peter Hobbing's chapter points out, there are serious doubts about the "technological build-up" around border security, the mass processing of personal data and the capacity of such approaches to be workable solutions for their intended public goals. As Hobbing argues, the issue is not just the impact on privacy, but also the ever-greater "risk of data leakage, erroneous results and painful consequences for the individuals concerned". The proportionality and efficacy of these approaches are questionable, especially in light of the economic repercussions of these kinds of technologies and their incapability of fulfilling the purposes they are meant to serve.

Over the ten years since the AFSJ was created, there has been a veritable explosion of development in the field of information technology.

What we are able to do now and indeed what we take for granted in terms of access to data on the Internet, the availability of information and its use was only barely within the dreams of a small number of experts a decade ago. While this extraordinary change in data availability has brought tremendous benefits to the EU, it also poses very serious issues for the present and future. The most important among these is the protection of privacy. This right, a core element of the EU Charter and the ECHR, has become a key feature of the constitutional framework of the EU. Yet, the mechanisms for protecting data about people individually and as groups have not kept pace with the development of technologies. All too often, EU regulation on data protection has accepted 'exceptions' to privacy rules on less than satisfactory grounds. Fears about political violence labelled as 'terrorism' and the privileging of some claims in law enforcement circles have to some extent unseated the principle of equality of arms between the prosecution and defence. The EU needs to find better mechanisms to ensure that individuals' data are not abused, shared with parties who are not entitled to it, only collected for legitimate reasons and subject to proportionality tests regarding retention. As the contribution by Joaquín Bayo Delgado underlines, in the next ten years the role of national courts in the EU data protection system will be central when redressing situations in which the result is an unacceptable infringement of the individual's right to privacy.

Asylum and fundamental rights

All EU member states are signatories to the UN Convention relating to the status of refugees (the 1951 Geneva Convention) and have reaffirmed their utmost commitment to the protection of all persons at risk of torture or inhuman or degrading treatment in their country of origin. The inclusion of international protection in the AFSJ has brought a new actor, the EU, to the field of refugee protection. This arena is already well populated at the international level. Not only are there three UN Conventions that all member states have ratified and which place protection obligations on signatory states (the Geneva Convention, the International Covenant on Civil and Political Rights and the UN Convention against Torture), there are also the institutional actors, including the UN High Commissioner for Refugees, responsible for a broad protection mandate. At the European regional level, the ECHR includes a duty of protection where there is a substantial risk that an individual would suffer torture, inhuman or degrading treatment if sent to a country. The European Court of Human Rights in Strasbourg has been vigilant in the protection of individuals from such risks. Into this crowded field the EU has now moved and taken its place. This step has not been without certain perils.

For instance, one of the core measures of the EU's Common European Asylum System is the Dublin II Regulation ((EC) No. 343/2003), which allocates responsibility for asylum applications and the care of the applicant according to specific rules that in practice usually means the country through which the asylum seeker first entered the EU is responsible. Because of the inadequacy of reception conditions in one member state (Greece), the constitutional courts of a number of other member states have halted any returns of asylum seekers there and the European Court of Human Rights has issued stays of return in numerous cases pending its examination of the situation. The EU needs to live up to its commitment to protect refugees and those in need of international protection. As the contribution by Madeline V. Garlick argues, the role of the Court of Justice in future decision-making on asylum after the Treaty of Lisbon could be crucial from this viewpoint. Any failure in this area will result in a serious problem for the legal coherence of the EU and deep damage to the EU's reputation as an actor in the field. How the EU lives up to its commitments with respect to refugee protection will be an important measure of its human rights credentials. This point is highlighted in the contribution by Jacques Barrot, who adds that

> the founding values of the Union, and our shared history of tragedy and reconciliation, in my view compel us to extend the hand of hospitality and solidarity with those facing persecution around the world. This for me is one of the greatest challenges, on a truly global scale, facing the future of European integration.

Cooperation in criminal justice and police

One of the most surprising aspects of the AFSJ has been the rapidity with which the EU has embraced judicial cooperation in criminal matters. This field is ring-fenced by national interests and differences, which most observers ten years ago thought would hamper cooperation very seriously. Yet in fact, tremendously important steps have been taken. Eurojust, the EU's body of prosecutors, has become not just a reality, but also a success far beyond the expectations of most observers ten years ago. As Hans G. Nilsson's contribution argues, merely the volumes of cases that pass through Eurojust and the coordination meetings that it organises indicate the significance of its work in the EU criminal justice systems. With the Lisbon Treaty comes the possibility of a new actor on the criminal justice scene - the European Public Prosecutor (EPP). While this new post is only enabled by the Treaty, it offers a tantalising possibility of greater coherence and cooperation in the field. At the moment it is clear that there are member states that are deeply suspicious of an EPP. Still, the Lisbon Treaty does provide the opportunity to use enhanced cooperation to start the project and thus to allow those member states that see added value in the project to try it out. This may in turn create a virtuous dynamic, in which the more sceptical member states may invest more heavily in the success of Eurojust as an alternative - in the end leading to greater consistency and coherence in criminal justice across the EU. The next ten years of the AFSJ as regards criminal justice will be critical to the EU's ability to work together and to provide a credible, joined-up criminal justice network if not system.

The ambitious JHA programme on judicial cooperation in criminal matters and in particular the European arrest warrant has raised new questions for national constitutional courts about the meaning of constitutionalism and their duty to protect the citizen. As discussed in Kristine Kruma's contribution, across the EU in member states that formed the EU in 1957 and some that joined in 2004, constitutional courts have been troubled by what has at times seemed a contradiction between their duty to maintain the highest standards of constitutional protection for citizens and to respect and obey the EU legal order. Constitutional courts are by their very nature actors of the Westphalian system - charged with a very specific role of protecting the individual against excessive incursions by state authorities within a strict jurisdictional framework. One of the most important subjects constitutional courts deal with is the state's use of violence within the jurisdiction - the arrest, punishment and imprisonment of individuals. The EU's embrace of the principle of mutual recognition as the mechanism to proceed in judicial cooperation in criminal matters has intensified the scrutiny some constitutional courts have given to the legitimacy of the EU's involvement at all. The use of mutual recognition has brought attention to the procedural practices of member states and their capacity to ensure the rights of individuals are safeguarded, such as those envisaged in the EU Charter, the ECHR and national constitutions. The new Lisbon Treaty setting will put to the test the capacity of the EU's courts to reinforce fundamental rights for individuals in the face of a state's claim to legitimacy in its use of violence.

The EU has entered the sphere of internal and external security as an important actor, although the definition of internal and external security remains a matter of deep uncertainty in an EU of 27 member states, each with its own understanding of the meaning of security. The Lisbon Treaty reinforces the role of all the EU institutions in security matters, a clear indication that the member states want a more coherent and transparent common approach. What remains unclear, however, are the kinds of actions and threats classified as internal security matters and in what context these are deemed internal. For instance, some member states have experienced internal security issues in the form of political violence. The continuing troubles in the Basque country are one example but are they an EU concern? Are they a concern of internal or external security? Among the issues that the EU institutions will need to examine are the relationships of various actions that have internal and external dimensions for the member states and for non-EU countries, including in the EU's neighbourhood policy and interests and claims regarding security. The arrival of the European Parliament as an actor in this important field of activity owing to the Lisbon Treaty is already changing the dynamic of the EU's security policies.

During the last ten years, the EU has also been very active in setting up mechanisms and structures outside the framework of the Treaties and in areas at the heart of national sovereignty. As demonstrated in the chapter of Johannes Vos, police cooperation is an excellent example of that. The development of Europol and the adoption of the Prüm Treaty are two paradigmatic instances of European cooperation falling outside the EU legal framework but of an intergovernmental nature, which have only subsequently been (partly) transferred to the EU setting and envisaged by the Treaty of Lisbon. As Vos says, 1998–2008 was "the creative phase" in police cooperation, with Europol being its main institutional arm. In the last decade, a new set of EU agencies in the area of internal security has emerged, such as the CEPOL (European Police College), Sitcen (Joint Situation Centre), the Task Force of European Police Chiefs and now the COSI (Standing Committee on Internal Security). The exchange of information among them is presented as central in the power struggles at the EU level and the current European internal security strategy. All these agencies and proposals will need to live up to increasing democratic control and accountability (including on the quality of the data exchanged) by the European Parliament and national parliaments. They will also have to work within a more consolidated framework of fundamental human rights, with agencies such as the European Data Protection Supervisor (EDPS) and the European Union Agency for the Protection of Fundamental Rights (FRA) becoming prominent actors in future debates and activities.

Conclusions

The EU's AFSJ constitutes the principal domain of the political elements of the European integration processes. It also plays a vital role in the added value and legitimacy of the EU for individuals (citizens and residents) in the Union as well as for 'the outside world' in a changing international context, in which EU AFSJ policies increasingly have external dimensions. This collective volume aims at contributing to the debates on the future configurations of the AFSJ. The experiences and views of practitioners and policy-makers are important to critical reflections on possible ways forward and to ensuring the relevance of any policy recommendation. The contributions in this volume offer unique input from this perspective. The Lisbon Treaty and the Stockholm Programme provide the institutional and political foundations for thinking about and proactively moving towards the next generation of the EU's AFSJ. This generation should be capable of satisfactorily enabling progressive Europeanisation (matching ambitions with practical outputs) along with a new supranational setting that is characterised by stronger democratic accountability, judicial control, efficient evaluation mechanisms for the full application of the rule of law and an ambitious, fundamental human-rights strategy.

2. THE EU'S AREA OF FREEDOM, SECURITY AND JUSTICE

SUCCESSES OF THE LAST TEN YEARS AND THE CHALLENGES AHEAD

JACQUES BARROT

Twenty years ago, the fall of the Berlin Wall marked a new era of freedom and solidarity for Europe. Today, as well as being the world's largest trading power with the second largest international currency and 500 million consumers, Europe is a place where people's rights are respected and their security protected. It is often far from clear however, whether Europe's citizens are fully aware of their rights and responsibilities, or whether they are fully empowered to exercise them. The Stockholm Programme is the EU's response to these questions.

There have been numerous successes to date. The extension of the Schengen area allows more than 400 million citizens to travel without border checks from the Iberian Peninsula to the Baltic States. Thanks to the establishment of Frontex, the Union's external borders are better managed. A common policy on asylum and immigration is being developed on the basis of efficiency and fairness. Through the European arrest warrant and facilitating the exchange of information among law enforcement authorities, we have built up our capabilities for fighting crime, and in particular organised crime and terrorism. EU civil and commercial procedures now make it easier for citizens and businesses to gain access to justice where they have a cross-border claim.

More work is now needed if the Union is to meet the challenges of the years to come. The coming into force of the Lisbon Treaty enables us to demonstrate greater ambition in responding to the day-to-day concerns and aspirations of people in Europe. Meanwhile, a greater role for the European Parliament will make the EU more accountable for its actions in the interests of the citizen.

The European Council sets out in the Stockholm Programme the priorities for meeting these challenges over the next five years. It is admittedly a dense document. Its contents reflect the discussions with member states, the European Parliament and stakeholders over the past year, but at its core are the ambitions the Commission outlined in its June 2009 Communication.[1] All in all, it amounts to a considerable mandate that will fall to Viviane Reding and Cecilia Malmström, the two commissioners who will take over from me and hold the reins of justice and home affairs (in a new era).

First, the programme will *promote fundamental rights* to help make European citizenship a tangible reality. The citizen's initiative provided for in the Lisbon Treaty is a powerful boost for European citizens' participation in the democratic life of the Union. Citizens should be able fully to exercise their rights to move to a member state other than their own in order to study or work, to set up a business, to start a family or to retire. With the increasing exchange of personal data, the Union must ensure that the right to privacy and principles of personal data protection are consistently applied. Attention must be given to the specific needs of vulnerable persons, particularly children and victims of crime. By acceding to the European Convention on Human Rights, the Union will both reaffirm – and bind itself legally to observing – its core values of respect for its citizens and their dignity. Once this happens, and it is my sincere hope that this will happen soon, European citizens who believe their rights to have been flouted will be able to bring their case before the European Court of Human Rights in Strasbourg. Freedoms and rights must also be protected beyond the EU's borders and in virtual environments such as the Internet. The Council has pledged to support the creation of a European certification scheme for 'privacy-aware' technologies, products and services. We will enhance consular protection so that any EU citizen who is in a country

[1] See European Commission, Communication on an area of freedom, security and justice serving the citizen, COM(2009) 262 final, Brussels, 10 June 2009.

where his or her member state is not represented can be sure of receiving his/her entitlements under the Treaties.

Rights come with responsibilities. The Council has signalled its commitment to increasing turnouts at European Parliament elections, including the possibility of the whole of Europe going to the ballot box on the same day - perhaps 9 May, the anniversary of the Schumann Declaration. Action in this area is of critical importance to the democratic legitimacy of the Union.

Safeguarding rights alone, however, is not enough. European citizens need to be empowered to invoke these rights wherever in the Union they happen to be. The second priority for the programme is therefore the development of a *Europe of law and justice*. There are still differences in guarantees provided to victims and these must be addressed. In the case of the accused, a clear 'roadmap' for progress in ensuring their rights are observed regardless of the member state in which they are to be tried has been agreed during the Swedish presidency. Clearly, in matters of criminal justice, the harmonisation of offences and sanctions will take time. Nevertheless, one of the great advances of the Stockholm Programme is that it opens the door for Europe to work together on detention conditions in prisons.

In the civil justice sphere, the cumbersome and costly *exequatur* process should gradually be consigned to history. Mutual understanding among professionals should be based on trust and the quality of justice, and the Union should work to eliminate barriers to the recognition of legal acts. We will continue work to increase access to justice through initiatives such as the e-Justice portal and greater use of video-conferencing technology.

If we are to achieve a genuine community governed by the rule of law, we must first foster greater mutual trust among judicial authorities. Training has a vital role to play. The Commission has advocated an ambitious target of at least 50% of all judges and prosecutors to have participated in a European training scheme or an exchange with another member state by 2014. The Council has in principle endorsed this vision. The Stockholm Programme also sets the objective of evaluating national justice systems. Judicial cooperation will be enhanced, based on the role of Eurojust, which may well evolve into a European public prosecutor.

Third, we envisage a *Europe that protects*. Globalisation means that the threats we face require concerted action at the European level. Our common threats of terrorism and organised crime, including human trafficking, child pornography, cyber crime, financial crime and drug trafficking, respect no borders and must be met with common policies and common tools. The exchange of information among member states' authorities on offences committed needs to become more efficient. We need a comprehensive system for obtaining evidence in cross-border cases. At an operational level, we need to remove the obstacles in the way of effective police action across borders. Europol will be given greater powers, and a network of police databases is envisaged. The programme moreover opens the way for a European internal security strategy, consisting of effective policies and common tools for addressing our common threats in order to protect lives and safeguard the freedom of our society. This strategy will bring together cooperation in law enforcement, border management, civil protection and disaster management along with criminal judicial cooperation with the aim of making Europe more secure. Finally, the Stockholm Programme looks ahead to the establishment of a European system of border guards to make our fight against trafficking networks and the human misery entailed more effective.

Fourth, the programme looks towards a *Europe of responsibility, solidarity and partnership in migration and asylum matters*. Our population is ageing, and the effective management of migratory flows is one of the greatest challenges facing the Union. Immigration has a valuable role to play in securing the EU's strong economic performance over the longer term. In an approach to immigration and asylum based on solidarity, we will seek to tackle illegal immigration networks, ensure the successful integration of legal immigrants and honour our obligation to provide asylum to victims of persecution. Since my appointment as commissioner for justice, freedom and security in May 2008, I have fought passionately for such a common system to be achieved by 2012. The economic downturn and rises in unemployment inevitably make member states more cautious in these matters. The Commission was not able to convince the entire Council of the need for an immigration code and for applying the principle of mutual recognition of decisions to grant international protection. Nonetheless, the need for the improved integration of new arrivals, refugees and regular migrants remains. Immigration enriches European society and strengthens innovation in our economy. Meanwhile, the founding values of the Union, and our shared history of tragedy and reconciliation, in my view compel us to extend the hand of hospitality and solidarity to those facing persecution around the world. This for me is one of the greatest challenges, on a truly global scale, facing the future of European integration.

Finally, the programme highlights the *role of Europe in a globalised world.* A robust external dimension to our policies will ensure consistency with the Union's foreign policy as a whole, and enable us to promote our values in compliance with international human-rights obligations. Effective engagement with our partners in non-EU countries and international organisations in the area of justice and home affairs will be essential.

This is our blueprint for developing the European area of justice, freedom and security in the years to come.

3. THE EUROPEAN COMMISSION'S NEW JUSTICE PORTFOLIO

OPPORTUNITIES, GOALS AND CHALLENGES

HASSO LIEBER

In September 2009, after long hesitation, the president of the European Commission, José Manuel Barroso, finally agreed to split up the justice, freedom and security portfolio and create a separate portfolio for justice when the new European Commission convened in February 2010. Countless politicians, legal experts and lobbying groups had called for this step. With the nomination of Luxembourger Viviane Reding as commissioner for justice, fundamental rights and citizenship, and the European Parliament's confirmation of the new Commission on 9 February 2010, the change is now complete. Berlin's Senate Department for Justice had advocated an independent justice portfolio since mid-2007, and despite strong opposition, was energetic in pursuing this goal in many different discussions with policy-makers, scholars, judicial officers and administrators in Brussels and Berlin.

Dramatic changes in EU justice policy

By making justice a separate area of responsibility, the Commission is acknowledging this area's increased importance. Once the smallest directorate-general, it has grown dramatically from about 90 employees to a staff of roughly 600. Comparing the multi-year Tampere Programme of 1999 with the Stockholm Programme adopted by the European Council in December 2009, which sets out guidelines for justice and home affairs through 2014, gives us a striking example of how this policy area has developed in the last ten years.

Ten years ago, who would have thought that today we would be on the way to full harmonisation of consumer rights and have a justice commissioner whose long-term goal is to create a European civil code? Or that we would be discussing a legal instrument in criminal law enabling requests for the gathering of evidence in any member state to be processed under the mutual recognition principle? In other words, EU legal policy has undergone dramatic changes, and the Treaty of Lisbon will promote even more innovations, especially in criminal law, since a qualified majority vote of the Council is much easier to achieve than the unanimity of member states required by the Treaty of Nice.

Balancing interests and ensuring transparent decision-making

Stakeholders in the area of justice and home affairs often pursue opposing interests, especially when it comes to the conflicting priorities of security and freedom. One consequence of 9/11 was the marked preference given afterwards to security interests. A prime example of this orientation was the Commission's 2007 proposal[1] - which was ultimately rejected - of a framework decision on using airline passenger data for law enforcement purposes. In the interests of security and combating terrorism, the commissioner for justice, freedom and security responsible for this policy area at the time, Franco Frattini, advocated the precautionary retention of all such data for a period of 13 years. Passengers would have had very few rights to notification, information, correction or deletion of the data that had been collected.

In the interest of a system of checks and balances, it was necessary to separate the Commission's areas of justice and home affairs. "*Que le pouvoir arrête le pouvoir*", and as the conflicts of interests discussed here make clear, Montesquieu's core idea of the separation of powers can be applied not only to the state's executive bodies but also to organisational issues within a single authority. The balancing of interests by means of reciprocal control is part of the separation of powers that already exists in all of the member states. The separation of justice and home affairs is the norm in 22 of the 27

---

[1] See European Commission, Proposal for a Council framework decision on the use of Passenger Name Record (PNR) for law enforcement purposes, COM(2007) 654 final, Brussels, 6 November 2007.

member states and can thus be considered the European standard, even though the areas included in each of the portfolios probably differ from one member state to another.

The separation will now become the standard in the EU, since there are good reasons why it has become a traditional part of today's governments. As we all know, political decision-making on basic issues and specific areas depends in large part on the point of view of the person making the decision. With that in mind, having two separate advocates at the highest level ensures a balanced approach to potentially explosive issues related to freedom and security. This promotes better decision-making and is crucial to citizen acceptance of sovereign policies, since an active exchange of viewpoints brings the discussion of pros and cons to the attention of the public, enhancing visibility and transparency.

Expectations of the justice commissioner

a) As might be anticipated, the newly established justice portfolio has overall responsibility for (almost) all legal policy issues. In particular, the draft directive on consumer rights that was the subject of impassioned debates in Council working groups and the Parliament has been transferred from the Directorate-General for Health and Consumers to the justice commissioner's portfolio. In view of the draft's profound potential impact on the civil codes of the individual member states, this change can only be considered a welcome step. Putting all legal policy issues in the hands of the justice commissioner will help to make legal instruments more coherent, an important goal. Against this backdrop, leaving the Directorate-General for Health and Consumers in charge of introducing class-action suits for consumers, a project currently in the planning stages, makes little sense; in the interest of coherent rules, the justice commissioner will need to work closely with the other directorate-general to coordinate content. Along with coherence, a key concern of EU legislation must be to balance various interests - one of the core tasks of a justice department in any democracy.

b) Past priorities are evident in the remarkable progress made in expanding on the mutual recognition principle in criminal law, with the aim of prosecuting criminals more effectively, while the establishment of uniform minimum protections for defendants in criminal cases is still at an early stage. There is reason to hope that having a separate advocate for the justice portfolio will help to redress this balance, since it is essential that we set high standards for defendants' rights after years in which legal security has been neglected in favour of domestic security.

c) With an independent focus on justice, data protection will no longer be regarded as just a security policy 'appendage'. We can assume that the proposed framework decision discussed above (on setting up an EU-wide system to retain airline passenger data) would not have been submitted in its original form, which showed a blatant disregard for data protection, if the Commission had already had a separate justice commissioner. If the Commission is going to make a second attempt at a proposal on setting up a system of this kind, it will have to be coordinated with the justice commissioner. She will ensure its commitment to both procedural and substantive legal standards under the rule of law.

d) Implementing the Common Frame of Reference for contract law, which was submitted by European legal scholars in November 2009, will present another challenge. There is general agreement that political leaders should push for a meticulously formulated European contract law. Yet, the actual form it should take and its legal force are still unclear; the current point of view – at least according to the Stockholm Programme – is that it should serve only as a source of inspiration for EU legislation. This attitude may change in the near future: at the confirmation hearing held for Justice Commissioner Reding by the European Parliament, Ms Reding voiced very ambitious goals for European contract law and described the Common Frame of Reference for European contract law as the "embryo" of an EU civil code. That means we can anticipate an exciting debate with wide-ranging consequences for European legal culture.

Outlook

With the division of responsibilities between two separate commissioners for justice and home affairs, we have, however, achieved only an intermediate goal, although an important one.

While the current organisational plan provides for separate leadership in the areas of justice and home affairs, the commissioners continue to share a single directorate-general. This structure is an obstacle to achieving the conflicting goals of justice and security; because of the shared platform, there is a real danger that justice policy interests will be 'filtered out' as they work their way through the department and never reach the justice commissioner. The areas of criminal justice and counterterrorism currently do not have their own advocates at the directors' level - a situation that is not conducive to achieving a more transparent Europe, which involves a serious and credible commitment to protecting civil rights. As a result, it is essential that a separate directorate-general for justice, fundamental rights and citizenship be created as soon as possible.

Along with the Commission, the Justice and Home Affairs Council also needs to be reorganised. Here, too, justice has long been subordinate to domestic policy issues. The communitisation of the 'third pillar' and the accompanying disentangling of security and justice policy interests makes it possible to imagine future developments here as well: holding separate council meetings, as well as separate preparatory meetings at the staff and ambassadorial levels, would make home affairs less dominant and increase the transparency of what are often conflicting interests. In this respect, it would also appear that the time is ripe for the genuine emancipation of justice at the EU level. This will be successful only if the justice ministers of the member states are able to take up European legal issues independently in their own council.

4. THE DEMOCRATIC ACCOUNTABILITY OF THE EU'S AREA OF FREEDOM, SECURITY AND JUSTICE TEN YEARS ON

EMILIO DE CAPITANI

Enhancing parliamentary oversight

It is common knowledge that national parliaments are the 'winners' in the institutional reshaping of the EU's decision-making process after the entry into force of the Lisbon Treaty.

The new chapter on democratic principles in the Treaty on European Union (TEU) and particularly Art. 12, stresses that national parliaments shall "contribute actively to the good functioning of the Union" by taking part in defining EU legislation and ensuring respect for the principle of subsidiarity in the matters of shared EU and member state competences. This indicates a strong willingness of all member states to increase democratic accountability in the continuing construction of the EU, as demanded by civil society and the German Federal Constitutional Court in 1993 with the Maastricht Treaty and more recently in 2009 with the Lisbon Treaty.

Seventeen years after the first declaration on national parliaments annexed to the Maastricht Treaty, followed by the entry into force of the Amsterdam protocol in 1999, national parliaments can now play a stronger role, notably in the Area of Freedom, Security and Justice (AFSJ). These policies should be established and implemented "with respect for fundamental rights and the different legal systems and traditions of the

Member States" (Art. 67(1), Treaty on the Functioning of the European Union, TFEU).

Consistent with this approach and with the need for national legislatures to maintain a strong role in the AFSJ, the Treaty has strengthened subsidiarity control and the 'alert system', as it can now be triggered by a quarter of the national chambers (instead of a third as foreseen in other EU policies). Moreover, national parliaments will also be associated with the European Parliament in the evaluation of AFSJ policies and their practical implementation, as well as the evaluation of the main EU agencies operating in this field, such as Europol and Eurojust (see Arts. 70, 71, 85 and 88 TFEU).

So far everything seems to be in place, at least at the level of the Treaties, to strengthen parliamentary oversight and specifically the contribution of national parliaments in developing the new phase of the AFSJ. Yet, the question remains of whether, in the real world, the principles will be truly realised.

Looking at the experience of the Committee on Civil Liberties, Justice and Home Affairs (LIBE), possibly the committee most involved in establishing AFSJ policies, it is clear that some improvements are still needed to close the existing gap between theory and practice. Much more should be done at the European and national levels to strengthen cooperation between national parliaments and the European Parliament, in order for parliaments to have a stronger impact when defining and implementing EU legislation.

In principle, the very idea of closer interparliamentary cooperation in the AFSJ, as foreseen in Art. 12(f) of the TEU, is shared by all the institutions involved and has been reiterated several times in recent years, not least at the "EU Speakers' Conference" in Stockholm on 14-15 May 2010.[1]

---

[1] See the document, "Presidency Conclusions" from the meeting, 14-15 May 2010 on the website of the Swedish Parliament (http://www.riksdagen.se/upload/Dokument/utskotteunamnd/200910/Talmanskonferens-20100514/EUSC_Presidency_Conclusions_final.pdf) and also "Background note: Evaluation and monitoring in the area of freedom, security and justice" on the same website (https://www.riksdagen.se/upload/Dokument/utskotteunamnd/200910/Talmanskonferens-20100514/Monitoring-freedom-security-and-justice.pdf).

The crucial point now is how to improve cooperation by taking stock of the experience we have had so far.

Indeed, when looking at the comparable interaction between EU institutions and civil society representatives, or at the thousands of lobbyists who regularly follow the legislative work, the cumulative role of the 40 national chambers looks rather solitary and seems to be facing some difficulties in keeping up with the rhythm of the European decision-making process. On a quantitative basis, hundreds of opinions of the national chambers have been adopted since the launch in 2006 of the parliamentary dialogue (the so-called 'Barroso initiative'). Yet, many of them have not had a real impact on the procedure for several (and sometimes trivial) reasons, such as opinions being sent only to the Commission and not to the other institutions, or reaching EU legislators after a political agreement had been reached on the topic, or referring to a text that was already outdated.

These shortcomings are frustrating, not least for the European Parliament, which is very keen on obtaining the positions of civil society and especially those of the national parliaments on the Commission and member states' proposals. An appalling example of how important cooperation could be between the European Parliament and the external world is the 10-year saga on data protection. It is evident that it would have been impossible for the European Parliament to establish an alternative strategy to that of the Council and Commission without the support of information obtained on these issues by the European and national data protection authorities. Yet (and quite surprisingly), it proved nearly impossible to establish such a dialogue with the national parliaments, even though in many cases the same issues were debated at the national level.

It is true that by adopting around 200-300 main documents per year, the EU institutions create a workload that is higher than that of a single member state in the same field. This can prove to be a real challenge for a national parliament that is (and obviously has to remain) mainly focused on national legislation.

That being said, it is also true that the EU agenda is rather predictable, as are the different steps in the EU decision-making process. This allows for the possibility for a national chamber to easily limit the scope of its intervention to the approximately 30-40 legislative procedures and the 10-15 strategic documents that fall into the AFSJ domain. By doing so, the rest of the workload could be shared with other national chambers and general issues could be dealt with in cooperation with other national parliaments.

It is clear that in a given timeframe more or less all the national chambers are faced with the same challenges, be it during the ascending phase of the decision-making process and when Art. 12 of the TEU is at stake, or even more so when the implementation deadlines in the national legislation of an EU measure are approaching. In an era dominated by the concept of sharing information and mutual support, it should be relatively easy to build on the existing information tools, such as IPEX,[2] as well as to create virtual spaces (for instance, an EU 'Wiki-lex' environment) where informal information could also be shared.

Undoubtedly, a cooperative approach could be extremely helpful when new legislative objectives are taking shape in EU strategic planning.

Strengthening the interparliamentary dialogue when AFSJ strategies are defined

The starting point of dialogue between the European and the national parliaments could be when "strategic guidelines for legislative and operational planning within the area of freedom, security and justice" are defined by the European Council (Art. 68 TFEU). Based on experiences so far, however, it is hard to say that the European Parliament or the national parliaments had the opportunity to interact in a fruitful manner or to influence the outcome of the European Council when it adopted the EU multiannual programmes in the AFSJ in 1999 (Tampere), 2004 (The Hague) or 2009 (Stockholm, ten days after the Lisbon Treaty entered into force). Moreover, the same applies when the anti-terrorism strategy (regularly updated since 2001), the European pact of asylum and migration (2008) or the EU drugs strategy were established.

Even if in some cases the European Council's deliberations were prepared by a Commission communication and these communications triggered the resolutions of some national chambers, it is not evident that the positions of national parliaments were taken into account by the European Council, as preparatory work is usually carried out under a rather blurred framework. Furthermore, it is not particularly reassuring

---

[2] IPEX refers to the website on Interparliamentary EU Information Exchange.

that the same frustrating experience has been shared by the European Parliament, which only found a clear reference to its own recommendations in some cases in 2004 and in 2009.[3] For those who consider these European Council strategies to be so general and consensual that it would be better to focus more on the implementing legislative programmes established by the Commission, it has to be remembered that the Commission has always fiercely defended its right of initiative. By doing so the Commission has maintained planning proposals already rejected by the European Parliament (such as the one on an EU passenger name record system) or taken years before submitting new proposals formally required by the European Parliament under Art. 192 of the EC Treaty (currently Art. 225 TFEU – see the request for a new legislative proposal on access to EU documents).

This experience shows that much more should be done by the other institutions and by parliaments themselves to obtain a bolder role when strategy is defined in the AFSJ. Looking at it from the viewpoint of the European Parliament, the first objective should be to oblige the European Council and the Council of the European Union to make their preparatory work more transparent. The fact that Art. 10 of the European Council's rules of procedure[4] makes reference *mutatis mutandis* to the provisions concerning public access to Council documents (set out in Annex II to the Council's rules of procedure) is very worrying. More specifically, the practice followed by the Council in the preparatory phase of its deliberations is highly unsatisfactory – be it when working in the legislative domains (only ministerial debates and votes that cover less than 10% of the institutions' work have to be accessible following the Council's interpretation of the new Treaty) or on strategic issues (where the Council considers that there is no transparency obligation).

---

[3] In 2004, under the Dutch presidency a reference was made to the need to activate the TEU Art. 67 'passerelle' bringing the co-decision procedure into several domains of the TEU Title IV. In 2009, a reference was made in the Stockholm Programme to the European Parliament's recommendation on the future EU judicial area.

[4] See European Council, Decision of 1 December 2009 adopting its Rules of Procedure, OJ L 315/51, 2.12.2009.

The question is therefore how to overcome the current situation, which did not improve even after the landmark ruling by the European Court of Justice in the *Turco* case.[5]

The key could be in the hands of the national parliaments, as it is more than likely that the lack of transparency in the preparatory work of the Council of the European Union (and European Council) is intended to notably protect the so-called 'space to think'[6] of the member states' representatives.

These member state representatives are also accountable before their national parliaments. Thus, the easiest way to break the current de facto *conventio ad excludendum* of the European and some national parliaments could be for the national parliaments to share among themselves and the European Parliament the information/preparatory texts of general interest (keeping away from documents that cover a specific national interest or are linked to the exclusive relations between a government and its own national parliament).

Sharing, in real time, such preparatory information and texts would also be consistent with the spirit of the Treaties, which develop a consistent parliamentary oversight. This is particularly true for the AFSJ, where the Treaty itself requires that European and national parliaments be associated with the evaluation of AFSJ policies:

> Without prejudice to Articles 258, 259 and 260, the Council may, on a proposal from the Commission, adopt measures laying down the arrangements whereby Member States, in collaboration with the Commission, conduct objective and impartial evaluation of the implementation of the Union policies referred to in this Title by Member States' authorities, in particular in order to facilitate full application of the principle of mutual recognition. *The European Parliament and national parliaments shall be informed of the content and results of the evaluation.* (Art. 70 TFEU, emphasis added)

---

[5] Refer to Joined Cases C-39/05 P and C-52/05 P, *Kingdom of Sweden* and *Maurizio Turco v. Council of the European Union.*

[6] This expression covers the preparatory phase of Commission and Council decision-making as referred to in Art. 4 of Regulation No. 1049/01 on access to European Parliament, Council and Commission documents.

Taking into consideration this very wording of Treaty, how can the evaluation of the current AFSJ policies be separated from parliamentary participation in the re-definition of the same policies, particularly when shortcomings are detected and require prior amendment to the existing legal and operational framework?

This 'interparliamentary' oversight approach is further developed in the Treaties, especially by

- Art. 71, which grants national parliaments and the European Parliament the right to be informed of the activities of the Council committee in charge of the coordination of the action of member states' competent authorities operating in the internal security domain; and
- Arts. 85 and 88 of the TFEU referring to parliamentary control of Eurojust and Europol respectively.

Conclusions

Bearing in mind all these aspects, in its recommendations of November 2009 to the European Council on the Stockholm Programme, the European Parliament called

> for the creation of the evaluation system to give Parliament and national parliaments access to information related to the policies (Article 70 of the TFEU) and activities of the internal security committee (Article 71 of the TFEU) as well as of EUROPOL (Article 88 of the TFEU) and Eurojust (Article 85 of the TFEU), together with the European Agency for the Management of Operational Cooperation at the External Borders of the Member States of the European Union (Frontex), the European Asylum Support Office (EASO) and the Schengen system; considers, in this framework, that Parliament should be granted the right to deliver a binding opinion on the appointment of the agencies' directors (as Parliament is also the budgetary authority).[7]

[7] See European Parliament, Resolution of 25 November 2009 on the Communication from the Commission to the European Parliament and the Council – An area of freedom security and justice serving the citizen – Stockholm programme, P7_TA-PROV (2009) 0090.

In addition, the European Parliament considered that

> in order to frame Parliament's cooperation with national parliaments within the AFSJ, it would be worth creating a permanent forum of representatives at political level (two per Chamber + two substitutes) meeting twice a year and sharing a common workspace where all the information dealing with the AFSJ, including that of a restricted nature, could be shared in real time); considers also that the representatives of the national parliaments should be allowed to attend Parliament's proceedings at committee level and during Parliament's annual debate on the progress of the AFSJ.[8]

So far, quite surprisingly, national parliaments have not reacted to these ambitious European Parliament proposals and even if they consider that the AFSJ policies remain a high priority for parliamentary cooperation, the concrete forms of the cooperation are still to be defined.

Unfortunately, ten years after the Tampere Programme, we are still missing a common 'space to think' among parliaments in the EU. This is rather worrying when, for instance, after the entry into force of the Lisbon Treaty, in five-year's time the EU will be called to reshape the *acquis* of the former 'third pillar' and define its internal security strategy. Therefore, by acting alone the national parliaments risk missing the opportunity to shape future policies in this domain and the European Parliament itself will bear the responsibility of facing the Council, the Commission and even non-EU countries as was recently the case for the EU–US negotiations on the exchange of financial data (the so-called 'SWIFT' agreement).

---

[8] Ibid.

5. THE AREA OF FREEDOM, SECURITY AND JUSTICE AND THE ROLE OF NATIONAL COURTS IN THE EU DATA PROTECTION SYSTEM

JOAQUÍN BAYO DELGADO

The national courts play several roles in the EU data protection system, which can be summarised as follows:

a) As national data protection rules apply to courts themselves, courts have a basic role of applying data protection legislation to their own activities.

b) Criminal courts have a specific role in controlling the police application of data protection rules, when the police act as judicial police, and the respect by public prosecution offices of data protection legislation.

c) With the existence of a supervisory authority being a crucial element of the European data protection system, national courts have the role of revising the decisions of the respective national supervisory authorities.

First role

We have to consider the legal instruments applicable to courts in the European context. The first instrument, of course, is Art. 8 of the European Convention of Human Rights (ECHR). Although it refers to privacy, which does not coincide fully with data protection, it has to be remembered that privacy is a key right within the various rights covered by data protection legislation. The second relevant European piece of legislation is the Council of Europe Convention 108. In principle, all its provisions are applicable to all national courts, unless a party has made use of the derogations foreseen in Art. 9.2, which concerns the provisions of Arts. 5, 6 and 8,[1] or has under Art. 3 excluded certain areas from the scope of the Convention when ratifying it. France, Ireland, Latvia, Malta and the Netherlands have made use of such a possibility excluding some data pertinent to the areas of police and criminal justice.[2]

One area deserves special attention: the transfers of data to non-party countries, subject to the idea of adequate protection. In Convention 108, the only transfers covered are those among parties of the Convention under the principle of equivalent protection, as all parties, by the very fact of being under the Convention, are regarded as having equivalent protection. The Additional Protocol (Convention 181) has regulated international transfers to third parties, under the requirement of adequate protection, as in Directive 95/46/EC. Unfortunately, this Additional Protocol has either not been signed or ratified by Belgium, Bulgaria, Denmark, Finland, Greece, Italy, Malta, Slovenia, Spain and the UK.[3]

A third layer of legislation is comprised of the EU legal instruments and their transposition into national law. In this respect, the pre-Lisbon structure of pillars has produced two different legislative texts: Directive 95/46/EC and Council Framework Decision 2008/977/JHA. Superficially, it could seem that Directive 95/46/EC has no relevance for the Area of Freedom, Security and Justice (AFSJ), as it is basically a first pillar instrument. Indeed, the first indent of its Art. 3.2 reads as follows:

> This Directive shall not apply to the processing of personal data:
>
> in the course of an activity which falls outside the scope of Community law, such as those provided for by Titles V and VI of the Treaty on European Union and in any case to processing

---

[1] Austria has two interpretative declarations on Art. 9.

[2] See these exclusions and the limitations mentioned above, on the Council of Europe's website http://conventions.coe.int/Treaty/Commun/ListeDeclarations.asp?NT=108&CV=1&NA=&PO=999&CN=999&VL=1&CM=9&CL=FRE.

[3] This list was up to date as of 23 January 2010; see the Council of Europe's website http://conventions.coe.int/Treaty/Commun/ChercheSig.asp?NT=181&CM=8&DF=4/9/2009&CL=FRE.

operations concerning public security, defence, State security (including the economic well-being of the State when the processing operation relates to State security matters) and the activities of the State in areas of criminal law.[4]

Nevertheless, many EU member states have legislated to include police and criminal justice, completely or partially, in the scope of the national legislation implementing the Directive. The result has been that most provisions of Directive 95/46/EC are also incumbent upon police and criminal justice. At this point, it has to be regretted that terrorism and 'serious' organised crime have sometimes been excluded, for example in Spain, even if they are in the scope of Convention 108 and the country has not used the exclusion possibility of its Art. 3.

As to Framework Decision 2008/977/JHA, after a lengthy procedure, progressively watering down the content and ambition of the original Commission proposal, the text as it stands now has a very limited scope as defined in its Art. 1.2 (namely exchanged data) and thus does not cover the so-called 'domestic data' (data collected in a member state and not received from others). Therefore, any other provision of the Framework Decision, unless expressly stated otherwise, has to be understood within this very limited scope. Additionally, member states have another provision that allows them to further limit the transposition of the Framework Decision, as it includes a fourth paragraph under the same Art. 1 as follows: "4. This Framework Decision is without prejudice to essential national security interests and specific intelligence activities in the field of national security."[5]

How far "essential national security" and "intelligence" can be stretched remains to be seen in the specific transposition by each member state. Let us hope that, on the contrary, member states are going to make use of the possibility foreseen in the fifth paragraph of this same Art. 1: "5. This Framework Decision shall not preclude Member States from

---

[4] See Directive 95/46/EC of the European Parliament and of the Council of 24 October 1995 on the protection of individuals with regard to the processing of personal data and on the free movement of such data, OJ L 281/31, 23.11.1995.

[5] See Council Framework Decision 2008/977/JHA of 27 November 2008 on the protection of personal data processed in the framework of police and judicial cooperation in criminal matters, OJ L 350/60, 30.12.2008.

providing, for the protection of personal data collected or processed at national level, higher safeguards than those established in this Framework Decision."

While paragraph 4 makes it possible to broaden exclusions of data under the national legislation transposing the Framework Decision, paragraph 5 allows the application of data protection safeguards to areas not covered, thus including domestic data. But here we can have perverse effects. Let us imagine that a member state has applied Directive 95/46/EC to either police or criminal justice (or both) with no major exceptions as to the rights of individuals. As the level of protection set up in the Framework Decision is clearly lower than in the Directive (and unfortunately, than in Convention 108), including domestic data might mean reducing the level of data protection in the areas of police and criminal justice. On the other hand, if these areas are not covered by national legislation pursuant to Directive 95/46/EC or are covered by lower standards, the transposition of the Framework Decision to cover domestic data might produce a positive effect.

Furthermore, terrorism cannot be considered to fall under the exceptions of "essential national security" or "intelligence" because most of the reasons to adopt European legislation in the areas of police and criminal justice cooperation relate to terrorism and organised crime. The Framework Decision is the necessary instrument to guarantee a minimum level of data protection in that context of exchange of data. If terrorism were excluded nationally, the main purpose of this framework decision would be undermined.

With this legal panorama in mind, national courts, in both investigating crimes (in countries where the *juge d'instruction* exists) and in their proceedings and sentences have to respect privacy and other fundamental rights (the right of defence, non-discrimination, presumption of innocence, etc.) when applying criminal law. Higher courts have to review the application by lower courts as part of the legality they have to respect and guarantee.

The Framework Decision has a specific provision reflecting the principle of independence of judges, which implies self-control on the part of the judicial system. The provision refers to the rights of rectification, erasure and blocking, but it can be applied to the right of access as well:

Article 4 Rectification, erasure and blocking

4. When the personal data are contained in a judicial decision or record related to the issuance of a judicial decision, the rectification, erasure or blocking shall be carried out in accordance with national rules on judicial proceedings.

Another provision has to be mentioned, as it fills the hole left by the lack of ratification of Convention 181 (see above) in the area of transfers to non-party countries, yet only partially, as onward transfers are covered but not transfers of domestically obtained data. Art. 13 regulates these onward transfers although not in a very satisfactory way, as it includes too many exceptions to the principle of adequate level of protection in the receiving country or international organisation.

Finally, Framework Decision 2008/977/JHA includes a provision that allows the transmission of data to private parties, for example in the defences of subjects concerned by the proceedings. Art. 14.1(c)(i) foresees "the performance of a task lawfully assigned" to the private party as legitimate grounds to give access to data.

Second role

Criminal courts, as noted earlier, have the role of making sure that in the investigation phase the data protection legislation has been respected. If not, rectifications have to be made, or if the breach affects the principles of the abovementioned Art. 8 ECHR or other fundamental provisions such as Art. 6 ECHR (due process), the nullity of proof can be envisaged.

The legal panorama described above is basically the same to be applied to the police and the public prosecutor, given that from the EU perspective they are also included in the former third-pillar area. But the role of control of the judiciary needs a further nuance. Criminal courts can only supervise data protection aspects in the specific cases that reach the courts, not the general respect of data protection by police[6] or prosecution authorities. Normally, the national supervisory authority will be competent to supervise the respect of data protection in the performance of such general activities of the police and public prosecution offices. This leads us to the third role of national courts.

---

[6] Even a further distinction must be made for police, as in many countries the police also play an administrative role, for example in issuing passports and national identity cards. In these cases, criminal courts have no competences.

Third role

The setting up of one or several supervisory authorities is the subject of Art. 25 of Framework Decision 2008/977/JHA: "1. Each Member State shall provide that one or more public authorities are responsible for advising and monitoring the application within its territory of the provisions adopted by the Member States pursuant to this Framework Decision. These authorities shall act with complete independence in exercising the functions entrusted to them."

The next paragraphs of Art. 25 establish the powers of such authorities. Note that these powers are parallel to the existing ones under Directive 95/46/EC, but member states may choose to set up different authorities for police or criminal justice, which vary from those already existing. Let us hope that this will not be the case, as it is important to have a global and horizontal approach to data protection in all areas. Remember that under the Framework Decision, the existence of a supervisory authority is not mandatory for domestic data (being out of its scope), so there is no EU constraint on having a data protection authority for criminal domestic data. Fortunately, countries that have ratified Council of Europe Additional Protocol 181, which includes this aspect, are obliged to have a supervisory authority. In practice, though, here the problem is not so critical as in the area of transfers to non-party countries, as the existing authorities under Directive 95/46/EC are usually competent in the AFSJ.

So the courts become competent for appeals against decisions of the supervisory authorities. In this situation, it is not the criminal but the administrative[7] branch of the judiciary that is the competent judicial authority to review the decisions taken by supervisory authorities.

Both Directive 95/46/EC (in its Art. 22) and Framework Decision 2008/977/JHA (in its Art. 20) foresee a judicial remedy after the claim before the administration. Art. 17.3 of the latter includes a specific provision on the right of access.

---

[7] This point applies whether the administrative branch is structured within the judiciary or as a parallel branch, as in the French or Belgian system.

Looking ahead

The Treaty of Lisbon itself does not change the roles of national courts or the legislation they have to apply to themselves and to other stakeholders in the AFSJ. But as Art. 16 of the Lisbon Treaty does not make any distinctions among pillars,[8] domestic data in the AFSJ will have to be included in the revision of Framework Decision 2008/977/JHA, thus covering the entire scope of data processed by criminal courts, police and public prosecutors, even taking into account the specificities that Declarations 20 and 21 point out for the AFSJ. Therefore, the main recommendations for the future are as follows:

1) All EU member states should ratify Council of Europe Convention 181.
2) Terrorism and organised crime should not be excluded, by any means, from the scope of transposition of Framework Decision 2008/977/JHA.
3) The scope of Framework Decision 2008/977/JHA must be enlarged to include domestic data.
4) Member states should not reduce their present levels of protection that apply to AFSJ matters in their transposition of Framework Decision 2008/977/JHA.
5) On the contrary, they should use its Art. 1.5 to reach higher levels.
6) The rules on onward transfers under Framework Decision 2008/977/JHA should be modified to reach at least the levels of protection specified by Directive 95/46/EC.

National courts should continue to apply data protection rules in all proceedings and investigations, taking coherent decisions with respect to any breaches committed, even by annulling proof when proportionate.

---

[8] Art. 39 of the Treaty on European Union deals with the former second pillar, common foreign and security policy, which does not affect our analysis.

6. CONSTITUTIONAL COURTS AND THE LISBON TREATY

THE FUTURE BASED ON MUTUAL TRUST

KRISTINE KRUMA

Introduction

The snowball of Lisbon has started rolling. In February 2010, the constitutional courts (CCs) received a letter from the Belgian CC stating that the courts of other member states are invited to draw particular attention to a question referred by the Belgian Court to the European Court of Justice (ECJ) for a preliminary ruling.[1] The question referred is not linked to justice and home affairs (JHA) issues but concerns the exclusive competence of the CC to review the law for compatibility with the national constitution and the so-called 'concurrence of fundamental rights'. One can expect more cases appearing given that the Lisbon Treaty (the Treaty on the Functioning of the EU, TFEU) has brought significant changes in the JHA domain, which had been considered reserved to the state and the protection of its citizens.

---

[1] See Case C-457/09, *Claude Chartry v. Etat Belge*, lodged on 23 November 2009. The Court's representatives drew attention to several cases of the ECJ related to the judgement of 9 March 1978 in Case 106/77, *Simmenthal* [1978] ECR 629, for instance, the judgement of 27 June 1991 in Case C-348/89, *Mecanarte* [1991] ECR I-3277.

This can be regarded as a new starting point for clarifying the relationship between the CCs and the ECJ in the post-Lisbon era. The hypothesis discussed in this chapter is that the situation in relation to a *Solange*-type relationship between the CCs and the ECJ has changed, and enlargement has facilitated the process by bringing in new judicial institutions that might invoke the ECJ in a different legal–political context.

As argued by de Witte, there are three challenges that the EU places before national constitutional systems.[2] The first is the transfer of some law-making to the EU level. The second concerns the direct effect on and primacy over conflicting national law, and the third is related to a reshuffling of the internal institutional balance within each member state.

To prove the hypothesis, cases on the European arrest warrant (EAW) and national constitutional issues provoked by the Lisbon Treaty are analysed. The CCs of the **Czech** Republic,[3] **Germany** and **Poland**, as well as the Supreme Court of **Cyprus**[4] have reacted to the EAW, while the **Czech**,[5] **Spanish**,[6] **German**,[7] **Latvian**[8] CCs and **French** Constitutional Council[9] have

---

[2] See B. de Witte, "The Lisbon Treaty and National Constitutions", in C. Closa (ed.) *The Lisbon Treaty and National Constitutions. Europeanisation and Democratic Implications*, RECON Report No. 9, Arena Report No. 3/09, Arena, Oslo, 2009, pp. 26-27.

[3] Refer to the Decree of the Czech Constitutional Court issued on 3 May 2006 (ref. Pl.US 66/04) stating the conformity of articles on the EAW with the local constitution. The key measure of the Czech legislation was the second sentence of Art. 14(4) of the Charter of Fundamental Rights and Basic Freedoms, according to which the citizen cannot be forced to leave his/her homeland.

[4] In its decision of 7 November 2005 (ref. 294/2005), the Supreme Court of Cyprus asserted that the act implementing the EAW is inconsistent with the constitution because the latter includes an unconditional ban on the extradition of Cypriot citizens in Art. 11(2). A summary is available in English on the Eurowarrant.net website (http://www.eurowarrant.net).

[5] See Czech CC judgements Pl.US 19/08 of 26 November 2008 and Pl.US 29/09 of 3 November 2009.

[6] Refer to Declaration 12/2004, DTC 1/2004, 13 December 2004.

[7] See judgement no. 2 BvE 2/08 and 5/08, 2 BvR 1010/08 and 1022/08 and 1259/08 and 182/09, 30 June 2009.

[8] See judgement no. 2008-35-01, 7 April 2009.

[9] Refer to Decision No. 2007-560 DC, 20 December 2007.

delivered rulings on either the Constitutional Treaty or Lisbon Treaty. The Czech Court has even been approached twice. The conclusions reflect on the Stockholm Programme and the problems envisaged.

Transfer of competences

Although the JHA domain has so far functioned on the basis of intergovernmental cooperation, the EU institutions have been active and have adopted instruments provoking reactions from the CCs or other highest courts in the member states. The implementation of the Stockholm Programme may give rise to an increase in such reactions. Thus, it is important to establish the red lines set by the various CCs. The first to mention have emerged from the EAW cases.

The **Spanish** CC pronounced its view on the extradition of nationals even before the EAW had been adopted. It referred to Art. 7 of the Dublin Convention of 1996 and stated that "under no circumstances can the extradition of nationals to countries that have signed the European Convention on Human Rights (ECHR) give rise to general suspicions of failure to fulfil a state's obligations to guarantee and safeguard its nationals' constitutional rights".[10] The **Czech** Court agreed with the **Spanish** position when approached by members of parliament. They claimed that the constitution prohibits citizens from being forced to leave their homeland and to be prosecuted for acts that are not defined as criminal in Czech Republic. The Court argued that surrender is limited in time for the purposes of criminal prosecution and that there is no doubt about the permanent relationship between a citizen and the state. Thus, the Czech Republic is merely assisting the other member state with the enforcement of that state's criminal law.[11] The **Belgian** Court decided to ask

---

[10] See the Decision by the Constitutional Court, First Chamber, 27 March 2000, 87/2000, *Official Gazette* 107, 4.5.2000 (http://codices.coe.int, ESP-2000-1-012).

[11] The surrender of a person to another EU member state for prosecution will be a matter for consideration only where the conduct constituting a criminal offence did not occur in the Czech Republic but in another member state. See 3 May 2006, Pl.US 66/04, *Official Gazette* 434/4006 (http://www.codices.coe.int, CZE-2006-2-006).

for a preliminary ruling and the interpretation of the ECJ was reproduced in the Belgian decision.[12] This quite open and liberal approach was not upheld by other CCs.

Although not unanimously, the **German** CC dealing with the EAW concluded that it was the national law implementing the framework decision that infringed certain principles of the German Basic Law, such as proportionality and the guarantee of legal protection.[13] The competence of the European Community was not disputed, since Germany has ratified the Nice Treaty and this has not led to a loss of the core elements of statehood. Still, the EAW encroached upon the freedom from extradition in a disproportionate manner. Thus, the interests of German citizens have not been taken into account.[14] Similarly, the **Polish** Court in its ruling on the EAW noted that the obligation to implement framework decisions is a constitutional requirement.[15] Nevertheless, this obligation might create conflicts with the national constitution. The Court went further than its German counterpart by declaring the EAW itself to be incompatible with the constitution, but deferred the time for the constitution to be amended by 18 months. These CCs showed bias and distrust in the proper application of the EAW in another EU member state compared with the **Czech** and **Spanish** Courts.

---

[12] Yet another approach emerged when the Belgian Arbitration Court was approached by a non-profit-making association regarding the legality of Framework Decision 2002/584/JHA on the EAW and the Court referred relevant questions to the ECJ rather than evaluate the constitutionality of the EAW by itself. See the Belgian Court of Arbitration, 13 June 2005, *Official Gazette* 124/2005, 1.8.2005 (http://www.codices.coe.int, BEL-2005-2-011). For the response of the ECJ, see the judgement of 3 May 2007 in Case C-303/05, *Advocaten voor de Wereld VZW* [2007] ECR I-3633. The CC reproduced paras. 45 to 60 of the ECJ judgement in its own decision. See Constitutional Court, 10 October 2007, *Official Gazette* 128/2007, 24.10.2007 (http://www.codices.int, BEL-2007-3-008).

[13] See the judgement of the Second Senate of 18 July 2005, 2 BvR 2236/04.

[14] A number of dissenting opinions were attached to the judgement, some regretting that the Senate had refused to make a positive contribution to European solutions, and that by declaring the national act implementing the framework decision void, the Court was over-emphasising the role of citizenship and proportionality. See especially the dissenting opinions of Judges Lübbe-Wolff and Gerhardt.

[15] See Case P 1/05, 27 April 2005.

Apart from the EAW there have been other cases dealt with by the CCs. For instance, the **Hungarian** Court has dealt with the case upon application of the president concerning an agreement between the EU and Iceland and Norway on surrender procedures.[16] The Court found that a treaty provision precludes the executing state from determining whether the offence in question constitutes an offence under national law. Additionally, the double criminality provision was found to be contrary to Hungarian law. Separate and dissenting opinions were attached to the ruling appealing to mutual trust and confidence in other legal systems.

Different CCs have dealt with the transfer of competences related to JHA in the context of the Lisbon Treaty. The **Czech** Court has dealt with the compatibility of Art. 83 TFEU with the constitution in two rulings. The same article has also been discussed by the **German** CC from the point of view of history, values and traditions. The **German** CC noted that the Lisbon Treaty considerably extends the EU's competences in the area of administration of criminal law. Although both CCs were mindful of existing ECJ case law, the German CC observed that criminal law has always been a central duty of the state authority and is anchored in its values.[17] The **Czech** Court placed emphasis on the present day realities of growing mobility and cooperation, which require trust among EU member states. The Court said it has no doubts about the standard of protection of fundamental rights in the EU in this regard.[18]

The **German** and **Czech** CCs acknowledged that the integration of the state into the EU may require agreement to cooperate on matters with a cross-border dimension.[19] The German CC noted, however, that the interpretation of this mandate would be strict and require particular justification. Moreover, a veto provided by the Lisbon Treaty might be

---

[16] See Constitutional Court, 12 March 2008, 32/2008, *Official Gazette* 2008/40 (http://www.codices.coe.int, HUN-2008-1-001).

[17] See note 7 *supra*, paras. 352 and 355. The German Court referred to the judgement of 13 September 2005 in Case C-176/03 *Commission v. Council* [2005] ECR I-7879. See also note 5 *supra* Pl.US 29/09, paras. 157–158. The reference was made to case C-176/03 and the judgement of 23 October 2007 in Case C-440/05, *Commission v. Council* [2007] ECR I-9097.

[18] See para. 155 of judgement Pl.US 29/09.

[19] See note 7 *supra*, para. 357. See also note 5 *supra*, Pl.US 19/08, para. 170 and Pl.US 29/09, paras. 130, 145 and 156.

invoked if fundamental aspects of its criminal justice system are affected.[20] The German Court placed an obligation on its representatives in the Council to ensure the adoption of only the minimum rules with regard to the definition of especially serious crimes with a cross-border element and sanctions only to the extent essential to ensure the effective implementation of a Union policy.[21] In addition, German representatives will have to acquire a mandate from the German Bundestag, and if necessary the Bundesrat, to adopt decisions under Arts. 82(3), 83(3) and 86 TFEU.[22]

The differences in approach of the CCs are multifaceted. The EAW can be considered a litmus test for mutual trust between the judiciaries of the member states and the ECJ. This issue will remain relevant in the context of both the Lisbon Treaty and implementation of the Stockholm Programme.

Primacy of EU law

The Lisbon Treaty has offered a possibility for CCs to take a fresh or even first look at their debates on primacy, how the EU is defined in this context and what the limits are to the primacy of EU law.

The **Czech** and **Latvian** Courts have noted that the transfer of powers cannot go so far as to violate the very essence of the republic as a sovereign and democratic state governed by the rule of law and founded on respect for human rights.[23] Yet both courts departed from the theory of 'final say'

---

[20] See note 7 *supra*, para. 358.

[21] Ibid., paras. 361-362 and 364.

[22] Ibid., para. 365.

[23] See Pl.US 19/08, para. 97, note 8 *supra* and para. 18.2. Yet, the Czech Court noted that in cases Pl.US 19/08 and Pl.US 66/04, the Court had implicitly admitted that the CC should have an opportunity to examine European legal provisions in terms of their conformity with the constitutional order as a whole and not just with the essential core. In such a review it can then define those provisions of the constitutional order that cannot be interpreted consistently with the requirements of European law by using a domestic methodology, and which it would be necessary to amend. See Pl.US 29/09, para. 172. The Czech Court also refused to accept the president's concept of sovereignty, which provided that sovereignty cannot be restricted or shared or to create a catalogue of non-transferrable powers. The Court considered these issues predominantly political, which should be decided by the legislature (refer to Pl.US 29/09 paras. 62, 109 and 111).

advocated by Germany and adhered to the approach of 'initial say'. The initial say theory places emphasis on the aims, nature and structure of an organisation that is implementing competences. Thus, the transfer of certain competences to the EU must be regarded as an exercise of sovereignty of the people to reach the aims set forth in the EU instead of being considered a dilution of sovereignty.[24] Both CCs noted that the transfer of certain state competences - arising from the free will of the sovereign state and which will continue to be exercised with the state's participation in a manner that is agreed upon and subject to review - is not a conceptual weakening of sovereignty. On the contrary, it can lead to strengthening sovereignty within the joint actions of an integrated whole.[25] Particular emphasis was placed on the preservation of national identities along with political and constitutional self-government.[26] According to the **Spanish** Court, these precepts, among others, confirm the guarantee of the existence of the states and their basic structures.

Although issues concerning the protection of human rights were the main reason for the initial clashes between the ECJ and CCs, so far the Lisbon-related rulings have been quite limited based on the fact that the system will be changed. The **Czech** and **Spanish** CCs held that the protection of fundamental rights and freedoms falls in the area of the 'material core' of the national constitutions. It was also admitted that at an abstract level it is difficult to evaluate whether the individual rights and freedoms ensured in these systems are in harmony with each other, if these rights are not formulated absolutely clearly and in detail.[27] The **Latvian** CC noted that the Charter of Fundamental Rights and the ECHR, which would become binding for the EU under the Lisbon Treaty, are not incompatible with the constitution because all the documents are based on the same values and principles.[28]

---

[24] See note 8 *supra*, para. 18.3. The court was guided by *Affaire du Vapeur 'Wimbledon'*, CPJI série A, no. 1 15, 17 August 1923, 25.

[25] See note 5 *supra*, Pl.US 29/09, para. 147.

[26] Refer to Art. 4 of the Treaty on European Union, note 6 *supra* and note 8 *supra*, para. 16.3.

[27] See Pl.US 19/08, paras. 196-97.

[28] Moreover, the Court has repeatedly stated that the objective of the legislator was not to contrast the norms of human rights established in the constitution with international legal norms. See note 8 *supra*, para. 18.8.

The **German** CC observed that the state is neither a myth nor an end in itself but a historically grown and globally recognised form of organisation of a viable political community.[29] Yet, freedom of legislature is not unlimited. Limits are set by the condition that the sovereign statehood of a constitutional state should be maintained on the basis of an integration programme according to the principle of conferral and the member states' constitutional identity should be respected.[30] The Court went further to define core concepts by including, inter alia, citizenship and the civil and the military monopoly on the use of force, above all as regards intensive encroachments on fundamental rights such as the deprivation of liberty in the administration of criminal law or placement in an institution.[31] According to the German Court, especially sensitive for the state are decisions on criminal law, the police and use of force in an interior context.[32] In this respect, a transfer of sovereign powers beyond intergovernmental cooperation may only be realised under restrictive preconditions on harmonisation for certain cross-border circumstances.[33]

The recent judgements show a considerable opening-up of certain CCs towards the EU. At the same time, this is not unconditional as one can read the importance attached to identity issues. Moreover, some CCs have defined the spheres that are of special importance from a constitutional perspective.

New procedures and institutions

The claims brought by Lisbon Treaty challengers to different CCs have contained arguments in relation to specific JHA instruments and institutions that might encroach upon sovereignty, including changes in decision-making procedures.

For instance, a **French** decision established that provisions transferring to the EU under the 'ordinary legislative procedure' powers inherent in the exercise of national sovereignty require a revision of the

---

[29] The Basic Law breaks with all forms of political Machiavellianism and with a rigid concept of sovereignty. See note 7, *supra*, paras. 219 and 223.

[30] See note 7, *supra*, para. 226.

[31] Ibid., para. 249.

[32] Ibid., para. 252.

[33] Ibid., para. 253.

constitution. The Constitutional Council specifically referred to the fight against terrorism and related activities, border control, trafficking in human beings and judicial cooperation on civil and criminal matters.[34] The same principle also applies in relation to the prospective establishment of a European public prosecutor.[35] Furthermore, the Council ordered constitutional amendments in relation to the possible option of an ordinary legislative procedure when deciding on certain aspects of family law, the introduction of a simplified revision procedure and the involvement of national parliaments.[36]

The **German** CC criticised the Lisbon Treaty at length for a lack of democracy.[37] The Court stated that the institutional recognition of member states' parliaments cannot compensate for the deficit in the direct track of legitimisation of the European public authority that is based on the election of members of the European Parliament.[38]

In contrast, the **Latvian** and **Czech** Courts adopted a more liberal approach by emphasising the increase in the role of national parliaments.[39]

---

[34] Refer to para. 18 of Decision No. 2007-560 DC, 20 December 2007. The Council also affirmed its decision on the need to amend the constitution because of the Treaty establishing a Constitution for Europe is relevant in relation to articles of the Lisbon Treaty that are identical (para. 21).

[35] See para. 19 of Decision No. 2007-560 DC, 20 December 2007.

[36] Ibid., paras. 23-32.

[37] It should be noted that the German CC limited the scope of the review of the complaint (see paras. 168-206 of the ruling, note 7 *supra*).

[38] Ibid., para. 293.

[39] See note 8 *supra*, para. 18.4. The Czech Court commented that the position of national parliaments will increase, which is a good sign (Decision Pl.US 29/09, para. 135). To strengthen its reasoning on democracy, the Czech Court even quoted a passage from the Opinion of Advocate-General Poiares Maduro of 26 March 2009, in Case C-411/06 *Commission v. Parliament,* para. 138. The first to be mentioned in this context is the public prosecutor (Art. 86(1) TFEU). In the first case before the Czech CC, the application of shared competences, subsidiarity and proportionality as well as the competence of the ECJ was disputed in relation to JHA. The Court overruled the claims, stating that for the time being it is satisfied with this institutional framework. See Pl.US 19.08, paras. 137-139. In contrast with the Polish Constitutional Tribunal, which expressly rules out the jurisdiction of the ECJ to evaluate the limits of the conferral of competences to the EU, the Czech Court refused to formulate this so strictly.

In relation to a simplified Treaty revision procedure under Art. 48 of the Treaty on European Union, the **Czech** Court commented that as yet there are no provisions in the legal order of the Czech Republic allowing implementation of such decision-making procedures. Nonetheless, the absence of procedures does not affect constitutionality and the Court will acquire competence to review only after procedures are adopted in a timely manner.[40]

The **Latvian** CC was faced with the question on the role of a public prosecutor and noted that it is only a possibility and that the decision will be taken unanimously by the Council and with the consent of the European Parliament. Thus, Latvia will be able to block the decision if necessary. Moreover, even if a European public prosecutor's office is formed, the national procedures will not be affected because the issues covered would relate only to the financial interests of the EU and to matters of cross-border importance.[41]

Therefore, the CCs remain sensitive to the institutionalisation of JHA. While currently the courts remain open, much will depend on the implementation of the Stockholm Programme in terms of setting up new institutions and attaching new competences to them.

Conclusions

Rephrasing the views of de Witte as discussed in the introduction, it can be argued that CCs are facing a dilemma in the context of JHA. On the one hand, they are asked to show mutual trust and to open up to cooperation on JHA. On the other hand, CCs remain the main actors standing against the devaluation of national constitutions. Limited amendments to the texts of constitutions by state legislatures or people in referenda place an excessive burden on constitutional courts. In certain cases, constitutions have not been changed since the countries joined the EU.

Although the logic behind the need for a strong JHA domain in the EU is evident from the perspective of the common market, several CCs have shown that they maintain a clear stance on protecting a Westphalian system, under which the protection of citizens is perceived to be of

---

[40] See Pl.US 19/08, paras. 165-167.

[41] See note 8, *supra*, para. 18.7.

paramount importance. This seems to be outdated taking into account EU integration and the fact that all member states are parties of the ECHR.

The difference in views among the CCs shows that the role of the ECJ will remain central. Uncertainties caused by ambiguous formulations, wide discretion left to member states and unclear aims in the JHA domain can be settled by the ECJ in cooperation with the courts of member states. Mutual trust, as advocated all through the Stockholm Programme, should also be applicable in relation to the judiciary. This will become especially important given that national courts will have the possibility to refer preliminary rulings on JHA issues.

Even if the Stockholm Programme concentrates on implementation and strengthening the existing arrangements, many of them may cause constitutional reactions. The establishment of agencies, groups and networks that may come up with different initiatives might have gone unnoticed by the CCs so far.[42] In certain cases, problems could arise because the voice of a particular member state might not be heard owing to the changes in decision-making. Finally, crucial questions may arise concerning the consequences of de-pillarisation, the introduction of the 'Community method' and adoption of the Charter of Fundamental Rights, as exemplified in Belgium.

---

[42] The CCs are usually acting post factum, i.e. when decisions have been made. Thus, at this stage CCs are not in a position to react on possible future decisions in the areas of extradition, the fight against terrorism, cooperation in civil matters, data protection or migration.

7. The Common European Asylum System and the European Court of Justice

New jurisdiction and new challenges

Madeline V. Garlick[*]

Introduction

In the area of asylum and refugee protection, the entry into force of the Treaty of Amsterdam[1] in 1999 represented a major political and legal step. The right to determine who enters and stays lawfully on state territory – including as a refugee or person otherwise recognised as being in need of protection – had traditionally been seen as a key element of state sovereignty. Asylum and refugee protection issues were among the most delicate and widely-debated political issues in many member states, notably following the conflicts in former Yugoslavia. By agreeing under Amsterdam to shift legal competence from the national level to the Community level, and to harmonise member state law and practice in this

* The author acknowledges the assistance of M., M.C. and P. Rechter in the preparation of this chapter.

1 See the Treaty of Amsterdam amending the Treaty on European Union, the Treaty establishing the European Community and related acts (Amsterdam, 2 October 1997), OJ C 340/1, 10.11.1997. The consolidated text of the Treaty on European Union (TEU) and the Treaty establishing the European Community (TEC) appears in OJ C 321 E/1, 29.12. 2006.

sensitive area, member states thus entrusted control of an extremely important subject to their collective decision-making processes in the Council and to the EU institutions.

The shift recognised the evolving context of the European Union's legal order and physical reality, in which free movement policies and the progressive dismantling of border controls between member states meant that asylum seekers in the Union could also more freely cross national frontiers. Harmonising national asylum laws and policies was seen as a way to limit the phenomenon of 'secondary movement', under which asylum seekers were considered likely to move to the member state(s) where they could enjoy the most generous conditions and greatest chances of recognition and legal status.[2] Harmonised laws and policies, according to this rationale, would reduce the incentive to move, and encourage asylum seekers to remain in the first state in which they had an opportunity to seek protection.

---

[2] The UNHCR draws attention to the fact that asylum seekers move for different reasons, and not merely in search of favourable conditions. Yet, the prior and ongoing discrepancies among conditions, asylum systems and outcomes in the EU continue to pose significant questions about the results of the harmonisation process, and the fairness and efficacy of a system that places responsibility in a significant proportion of cases on external-border member states. See European Commission, Communication on a Policy Plan on Asylum – An Integrated Approach to Protection across the EU, COM(2008) 360, Brussels, 17 June 2008; see also UN High Commissioner for Refugees, *UNHCR comments on the European Commission's Proposal for a recast of the Regulation of the European Parliament and of the Council establishing the criteria and mechanisms for determining the member state responsible for examining an application for international protection lodged in one of the member states by a third country national or a stateless person ("Dublin II") (COM(2008) 820, 3 December 2008) and the European Commission's Proposal for a recast of the Regulation of the European Parliament and of the Council concerning the establishment of 'Eurodac' for the comparison of fingerprints for the effective application of [the Dublin II Regulation] (COM(2008) 825, 3 December 2008)*, UNHCR, Geneva, 18 March 2009 (retrieved from http://www.unhcr.org/refworld/docid/49c0ca922.html); and also UN High Commissioner for Refugees, *The Dublin II Regulation, A UNHCR Discussion Paper*, UNHCR, Geneva, April 2006 (retrieved from http://www.unhcr.org/refworld/docid/4445fe344.html).

In the ten years since the decision to establish the Area of Freedom, Security and Justice (AFSJ), the European Court of Justice[3] has had the opportunity to date to contribute to the development of EU asylum law through only a limited number of cases. Following the Lisbon Treaty's entry into force at the end of 2009, however, it would appear that the scope and impact of the Court's activities in the field are likely to increase significantly in future.

In committing to "establish progressively an area of freedom, security and justice" under Art. 61 of the Amsterdam Treaty, the Council agreed within five years to adopt "measures on asylum, in accordance with the Geneva Convention of 1951 and the Protocol of 1967 relating to the Status of Refugees and other relevant treaties". These covered the following aspects:

- the criteria and mechanisms for attributing responsibility among the member states for determining an asylum claim;
- minimum standards for the reception of asylum seekers;
- minimum standards with respect to the qualification of non-EU nationals as refugees;
- minimum standards on procedures for granting or withdrawing refugee status;
- minimum standards on temporary protection; and
- promoting a "balance of effort between Member States in receiving and bearing the consequences of receiving refugees and displaced persons".[4]

Along with all other areas under Title IV[5] of the Amsterdam Treaty, the asylum provisions in Art. 63 were made subject to the jurisdiction of the European Court of Justice. The Court was empowered by Art. 68 TEC[6] to

---

[3] The Court of Justice of the European Union comprises the European Court of Justice, the General Court and the Civil Service Tribunal. Among these, all cases relating to asylum have been referred to or heard by the European Court of Justice (referred to hereafter as 'the Court' unless otherwise stated).

[4] See Arts. 63(1) and 63(2) TEC, OJ C 321 E/1, 29.12.2006.

[5] Refer to Title IV: Visas, Asylum, Immigration and other Policies related to Free Movement of Persons, TEC.

[6] Read in conjunction with Art. 234 TEC.

give preliminary rulings on the validity or interpretation of Community acts based on Title IV, on a question arising in a case pending before a court or tribunal "against whose decision there is no judicial remedy under national law". This meant that the Court of Justice would be able to provide interpretive rulings on EU asylum legislation that would bind the member states - but only when asked by national courts of last instance, and not by courts at lower levels. (This limitation of preliminary reference power to final courts was seen as a means of ensuring that asylum cases would not flood the Court, given their prevalence in many judicial bodies at the national level.)

With its explicit obligation to ensure that asylum measures would conform to the 1951 Convention,[7] the Amsterdam Treaty forged an essential link between the EU's legal order and the international legal framework for refugee protection. Its reference to "other relevant treaties" also incorporates by implication the provisions on asylum and *non-refoulement* - prohibiting the removal of individuals to countries where they would face torture, inhuman and degrading treatment or punishment - in the UN Convention Against Torture (CAT)[8] and the International Covenant on Civil and Political Rights (ICCPR),[9] as well as the European Convention of Human Rights (ECHR). Although all EU member states individually are party to these instruments, the effect of Art. 63 TEC was to incorporate them explicitly into the EU's asylum framework and protection obligations. The political significance of this move was emphasised by member states shortly after the Amsterdam Treaty's entry into force, when the Council met and adopted the Tampere conclusions. Those conclusions "reaffirm[ed] the importance the Union and Member States attach to absolute respect of the right to seek asylum", and confirmed that it had "agreed to work towards establishing a Common European Asylum System, based on the

[7] See UN General Assembly, Convention Relating to the Status of Refugees, 28 July 1951, United Nations, Treaty Series, Vol. 189, p. 137 (retrieved from http://www.unhcr.org/refworld/docid/3be01b964.html).

[8] See Art. 3 of UN General Assembly, Convention Against Torture and Other Cruel, Inhuman or Degrading Treatment or Punishment, 10 December 1984, United Nations, Treaty Series, Vol. 1465, p. 85 (retrieved from http://www.unhcr.org/refworld/docid/3ae6b3a94.html).

[9] Refer to Art. 7 of UN General Assembly, International Covenant on Civil and Political Rights, 16 December 1966, United Nations, Treaty Series, Vol. 999, p. 171 (retrieved from http://www.unhcr.org/refworld/docid/3ae6b3aa0.html).

full and inclusive application of the Geneva Convention, thus ensuring that nobody is sent back to persecution, i.e. maintaining the principle of *non-refoulement*". [10]

This connection between Community law on asylum and the international protection system was further strengthened in Declaration 17 of the Amsterdam Treaty, providing that "consultations shall be established with the United Nations High Commissioner for Refugees and other relevant international organisations on matters relating to asylum policy". This acknowledged the role of the United Nations High Commissioner for Refugees (UNHCR) as the agency entrusted with supervisory responsibility in respect of the 1951 Convention,[11] and further demonstrated the apparent commitment of the drafters of the Treaty to ensuring that the EU's asylum rules would be developed and applied in line with international refugee law.

Link between the European Court of Justice and asylum jurisprudence at the regional and international levels

Through these specific references to international and regional sources of law on asylum and refugee protection, the Treaty framework ensured that the European Court of Justice assumed jurisdiction over EU asylum law against a background of important and well-established international and regional principles of refugee law. In addition to guiding texts such as conclusions of the UNHCR's Executive Committee,[12] these include a developed body of international and regional jurisprudence. The extensive

---

[10] See Council of the European Union, Presidency Conclusions of the Tampere European Council of 15-16 October 1999, SN 200/1/99, Brussels, 16 October 1999, para. 13 (retrieved from http://www.unhcr.org/refworld/docid/3ef2d2264.html).

[11] According to its Statute, UNHCR fulfils its mandate inter alia by "[p]romoting the conclusion and ratification of international conventions for the protection of refugees, supervising their application and proposing amendments thereto" (Statute of the Office of the United Nations High Commissioner for Refugees, 14 December 1950, A/RES/428(V)). This supervisory responsibility is confirmed by Art. 35 of the 1951 Convention and Art. II of the 1967 Protocol.

[12] In Conclusion No. 25(XXXIII) 1982, the Executive Committee "[r]eaffirmed the importance of the basic principles of international protection and in particular the principle of *non-refoulement*, which was progressively acquiring the character of a peremptory rule of international law".

case law of the European Court of Human Rights (ECtHR), which is particularly relevant to all EU member states, addresses many aspects of member states' treatment of asylum seekers and other persons who may be at risk of persecution or serious harm if removed to other countries. Such sources are available to assist the Court in defining and interpreting the 'general principles of law' that guide its decision-making processes, which include respect for fundamental rights.[13]

This link between the Court's jurisdiction over EU asylum law and existing developed case law is particularly well illustrated in relation to the principle of *non-refoulement.*

Key ECtHR cases such as *Soering*[14] established the principle that a state may not remove a person where there were substantial grounds for believing there would be a real risk of exposure to torture, inhuman or degrading treatment or punishment in the receiving state. This prohibition on *refoulement* was found to apply even where s/he had committed a serious crime, or if his/her continued presence in the respondent state would be unconducive to the public good for reasons of national security, including in the context of the fight against terror.[15] More recently, in *Saadi v. Italy,*[16] the ECtHR affirmed the absolute nature of this prohibition. The ECtHR's approach has been consistent with that of the UN Human Rights

---

[13] As expressed in Art. 6(2) TEU, "[t]he Union shall respect fundamental rights, as guaranteed by the European Convention for the Protection of Human Rights and Fundamental Freedoms signed in Rome on 4 November 1950 and as they result from the constitutional traditions common to the Member States, as general principles of Community law". Within this framework, the European Court of Justice uses all treaties that the member states of the European Union have signed or participated in as interpretive tools for the content and scope of "fundamental rights", while holding the European Convention on Human Rights as a document of "special significance". (See Case C-4/73, *Nold v. Commission* [1974] ECR 491.) In the *Kadi and Al Barakaat* judgement of 3 September 2008 (Joined Cases C-402/05 P and C-415/05 P [2008] ECR I-06351), the Court affirmed that "[t]he Community judicature must…ensure the review…of the lawfulness of all Community acts in the light of the fundamental rights forming an integral part of the general principles of Community law" (para. 326).

[14] See *Soering v. The United Kingdom* (1/1989/161/217) [1989] 11 EHRR 439.

[15] See *Chahal v. The United Kingdom* (70/1995/576/662) [1996] 23 EHRR 413.

[16] See *Saadi v. Italy* (Appl. No. 37201/06), Council of Europe: European Court of Human Rights, 28 February 2008.

Committee in relation to the *non-refoulement* obligation under Art. 7 ICCPR,[17] and of the Committee Against Torture regarding Art. 3 CAT.[18]

Other asylum cases before the ECtHR have examined different aspects of asylum procedures and systems. In the case of *Gebremedhin v. France,* the ECtHR examined the nature of effective remedies, and concluded that states are precluded from removing a person who is awaiting a decision on appeal against a negative decision on his/her asylum claim.[19] In *Saadi v. UK,* it ruled on the lawfulness of detention for asylum seekers, finding that administrative detention could be lawful provided it satisfied tests of necessity and proportionality.[20] In *SD v. Greece,* it was concluded that poor conditions of asylum detention could constitute inhuman and degrading treatment contrary to Art. 3 of the ECHR. [21]

These decisions have thus established an important set of common principles, derived from a European regional instrument, which is binding on all EU member states in the application of their asylum law. This case law has taken on particular significance in the EU following the adoption of the Qualification Directive (2004/83/EC), which employs the wording of Art. 3 ECHR in its criteria for the grant of subsidiary protection under Art. 15(c).[22]

It is interesting to note that at the time of writing, a series of cases was pending before the ECtHR regarding the risk of Art. 3 breaches through actual or proposed transfers from other member states to Greece under the Dublin II Regulation ((EC) No. 343/2003). Applicants alleged in a number

---

[17] Refer to Human Rights Committee General Comment N. 20 (1992), paras. 2–3 and 8, as quoted in E. Feller, V. Turk and F. Nicholson, *Refugee Protection in International Law: UNHCR's Global Consultations on International Protection,* Cambridge: Cambridge University Press, 2003, p. 145, para. 207.

[18] See Feller, Turk and Nicholson (2003), op. cit., footnote 167, p. 161.

[19] Refer to *Gebremedhin [Gaberamadhien] v. France* (Appl. No. 25389/05), Council of Europe: European Court of Human Rights, 10 October 2006.

[20] See *Saadi v. The United Kingdom* (13229/03) [2008] 47 EHRR 17.

[21] See *S.D. v. Greece* (Appl. No. 5341/07), Council of Europe: European Court of Human Rights, 11 June 2009.

[22] See Council Directive 2004/83/EC of 29 April 2004 on minimum standards for the qualification and status of third country nationals or stateless persons as refugees or persons who otherwise need international protection and the content of the protection granted, OJ L 304/12, 30.9.2004.

of cases that transfers could result in their indirect *refoulement* from Greece to other countries where they would be at risk of persecution or serious harm, or of further removal to face persecution or serious harm, because of systemic weaknesses in Greece's asylum system. In some other cases, it was alleged that conditions in Greece could of themselves amount to inhuman or degrading treatment, attracting responsibility under the *non-refoulement* principle.

The fact that the ECtHR has become involved in adjudicating in what are reported, at the time of writing, as over 100 cases concerning application of the EU *acquis* is significant. Some observers have asked why these cases arose in Strasbourg and not in Luxembourg. One reason is likely to be the previous limits on national courts' power to refer preliminary ruling requests to the Court of Justice. Prior to the Lisbon Treaty, Art. 68 TEC meant that only courts of last instance had such power. Asylum cases relating to Dublin II, however, by their nature were rarely able to come before the highest national courts. The limited information available to 'Dublin' applicants regarding their rights, combined with extremely short time limits to challenge transfer decisions and barriers to obtaining legal advice, collectively mean that challenges in Dublin cases are often not pursued at higher judicial levels. As such, this severely limits the scope for such questions - which raise critical issues of procedural fairness and affect thousands of people - to come before the Court. It is hoped that the Lisbon Treaty changes (as discussed below) will address this problem to a large extent.

The first referrals to the Court of Justice on asylum

Following the adoption of the first asylum instruments as required under Art. 63 TEC, member states began to apply the directly effective regulations on Dublin II and Eurodac, and to enact domestic legislation transposing the various directives into national law. As these instruments have progressively been utilised at the national level, the first preliminary ruling requests have been made to the Luxembourg Court concerning asylum questions.

The first request, in the case of *Petrosian*,[23] the Swedish (Migration) Court sought the guidance of the European Court of Justice on interpretation of time limits for transfer as defined under Dublin II. This

[23] See Case C-19/08, *Migrationsverket v. Petrosian and Others* [2009] ECR I-00495.

relatively technical decision was followed shortly thereafter by a ruling on a request from the Dutch Council of State in the case of *Elgafaji*.[24] In that case, the Dutch court had sought an interpretation of the concept of "indiscriminate violence" in Art. 15(c) of the Qualification Directive, providing for the grant of subsidiary protection to individuals threatened by such violence in situations of internal or international armed conflict. The Court found that the degree of individual targeting that had to be shown to establish an entitlement to protection varied according to the level and scope or widespread nature of the violence. It also established that the criteria for granting protection under Art. 15(c) were not the same as those for granting protection against removal established by Art. 3 of the ECHR, which was found to correspond rather with Art. 15(b) of the Qualification Directive.

These rulings were significant as the Court's first forays into the interpretation of Community asylum law in its new area of jurisdiction under Title IV. Yet, in three subsequent requests referred in 2008 and 2009, the Court received its first cases addressing concepts in the Qualification Directive that were based on specific 1951 Convention provisions. As such, these are the first cases in which the Court has been asked to interpret *acquis* asylum provisions derived explicitly from the primary international instrument on refugee law.

The first of these, *Abdulla and others v. Germany*,[25] was ruled upon by the Grand Chamber in March 2010. In its decision, the Court addressed the circumstances in which refugee status could be considered to have ceased, in line with Art. 11(1) of the Qualification Directive and Art. 1C(5) of the 1951 Convention, including the relevance of claimed new threats of persecution or serious harm, and the standard of probability and burden of proof to be applied in such cases. The Court acknowledged in its judgement that the 1951 Convention "constitutes the cornerstone of the international legal regime for the protection of refugees", and that the Directive's provisions were adopted to "guide Member States in the application of that Convention". It also specifically recognised that the Directive must be interpreted in light of its own general scheme and purpose, "while respecting the Geneva Convention and other relevant

---

[24] See Case C-465/07, *Elgafaji v. Staatssecretaris van Justitie* [2009] ECR I-00921.

[25] See Joined Cases C-175/08, C-176/08, C-178/08 and C-179/08, *Salahadin Abdulla and Others v. Bundesrepublik Deutschland.*

treaties", and in a manner that "respects the fundamental rights and principles recognised in particular by the Charter".

In these pronouncements, the Court appears to affirm its intention in construing the asylum *acquis* to pay close regard to relevant international legal instruments. In answering the questions of the German Federal Administrative Court, however, the Court also supported elements of the Qualification Directive provisions that are not based on the 1951 Convention - finding among other things that international organisations may be able to provide protection against persecution, in a way that would justify the revocation of refugee status. This aspect of the Qualification Directive had been questioned by the UNHCR and others, including on the basis of international law. Its endorsement by the Court raises questions about the nature of the balance the Court will seek to achieve between *acquis* concepts and international obligations in future judgements. The direction of its future jurisprudence will thus be of great interest, bearing in mind also that the Court has in recent years affirmed that fundamental rights form an "integral part" of the general principles of Community law that it is bound to apply.[26]

Further opportunities to examine these questions will arise in the cases of *Bolbol v. Bevandorlasi es Allampolgarsagi Hivatal*,[27] referred by the Budapest Metropolitan Court as well as *Germany v. B* and *Germany v. D* and others[28] from the German Federal Administrative Court, both seeking interpretations of other Qualification Directive articles. In *Bolbol*, the Court is asked to provide guidance on Art. 12(1) of the Qualification Directive, derived from Art. 1D of the 1951 Convention, relating to the entitlement of Palestinians to refugee protection. In *Germany v. B*, the Court will pronounce its view on the exclusion clauses of the Qualification Directive, which are similar - but not identical - to the related provisions in Art. 1F of the 1951 Convention.

In all of the initial, preliminary reference cases above, with the exception of the *Petrosian* case on administrative time limits, the UNHCR

---

[26] Refer to *Kadi and Al Barakaat*, footnote 14 above.

[27] See Case C-31/09 and the Advocate General's Opinion of 4 March 2010.

[28] See Case C-57/09 and Case C-101/09 - preliminary reference requests published in OJ C 129/3 and OJ C 129/7, 6.6.2009.

has issued a statement in relation to the questions before the Court.[29] Still, unlike in some other national and regional jurisdictions, including the ECtHR, the UNHCR has not participated as a formal third party to the proceedings. Under Art. 23 of the Statute of the European Court of Justice, only EU institutions and the member states are entitled to intervene in a preliminary ruling procedure. Unless it takes part as a party in the proceedings before the national court, in countries where this is possible, the UNHCR thus lacks standing under the Statute enabling it formally to put its views to the Court to assist in its deliberations. While Declaration 17 of the Amsterdam Treaty, requiring EU institutions to consult with the UNHCR, could be construed as extending to the Court, this has not been seen as the basis for a right to intervene as a third party to date.

Given the importance of the questions under consideration for the future evolution of refugee protection and asylum law in the EU, the UNHCR has chosen to issue its statements on the preliminary reference questions in the form of public documents, available to all interested parties. In each of the cases heard so far, one of the parties has submitted the UNHCR's statement as part of its official documentation provided to the Court, increasing the likelihood that the UNHCR's opinion might contribute to informing the deliberations around the case.

Consequences of the Lisbon Treaty

Two of the many changes effected by the Lisbon Treaty are particularly significant for the Court's future decision-making on asylum.

The first of these is the expansion of the scope of the national courts empowered to request preliminary rulings. The Lisbon Treaty abolishes

---

[29] See UN High Commissioner for Refugees, UNHCR Statement on Subsidiary Protection Under the EC Qualification Directive for People Threatened by Indiscriminate Violence, UNHCR, Geneva, January 2008 (retrieved from http://www.unhcr.org/refworld/docid/479df7472.html); see also UN High Commissioner for Refugees, UNHCR Statement on the "Ceased Circumstances" Clause of the EC Qualification Directive, UNHCR, Geneva, August 2008, (retrieved from http://www.unhcr.org/refworld/docid/48a2f0782.html); and also UN High Commissioner for Refugees, UNHCR Statement on Art. 1F of the 1951 Convention, UNHCR, Geneva, July 2009 (retrieved from http://www.unhcr.org/refworld/docid/4a5de2992.html); and UN High Commissioner for Refugees, UNHCR Revised Statement on Art. 1D of the 1951 Convention, UNHCR, Geneva, October 2009 (retrieved from http://www.unhcr.org/refworld/docid/4add79a82.html).

former Art. 68 TEC, which limited the right to request preliminary rulings to courts of last instance - meaning that all national courts, and not merely the highest judicial bodies, will be able to make requests in relation to asylum, immigration and visa issues. This has the potential greatly to increase the number of rulings that will be requested, but also to extend the range and subject matter of questions that will be put to the Court. Questions and provisions that may previously not have reached the highest courts can now be sent by the judicial tribunals and courts, which are dealing with the bulk of appeals or reviews of negative first-instance asylum decisions. This could be the case, for instance, with regard to Dublin II cases that until now have not been heard in the European Court of Justice because of the short timeframes and narrow appeal rights under most states' Dublin II procedures, which may have prevented them reaching the highest level of domestic judicial structures.

In March 2010, the first preliminary ruling request from a lower court came to the Court, from Luxembourg. This request, the first relating to the Asylum Procedures Directive (2005/85/EC),[30] deals with accelerated procedures and effective remedies - issues of great procedural importance for the operation of lower-level judicial bodies. This could indicate that the extended scope for preliminary reference requests will contribute beneficially to a more accurate and consistent application of basic asylum *acquis* rules at a practical level.

The second major change is the conferral of legally binding effect on the EU's Charter of Fundamental Rights. Art. 18 of the Charter, providing that the right of asylum "shall be guaranteed with due respect for the rules of the Geneva Convention"[31] can consequently be invoked directly,[32] not only before the Court of Justice, but also at the national level. It is not clear how the Court will interpret 'right to asylum' or the nature of this 'guarantee', nor the interplay between this article and other provisions in

---

[30] Council Directive 2005/85/EC of 1 December 2005 on minimum standards on procedures in member states for granting and withdrawing refugee status, OJ L 326/13, 13.12.2005.

[31] Refer to Charter of Fundamental Rights of the European Union, OJ C 364/1, 18 December 2000.

[32] See M.T. Gil-Bazo, "The Charter of Fundamental Rights of the European Union and the Right to be granted Asylum", *Refugee Survey Quarterly*, Vol. 27, No. 3, 2008, p. 33ff.

the asylum *acquis*. Given that the Charter carries the same legal force as the Treaties, it should in principle prevail over any inconsistent provisions in an EU directive or implementing national law. This could potentially open the way for interesting and challenging legal arguments in a number of areas, including notably access to asylum procedures and to protection.

Similarly, Art. 19 of the Charter, affirming the principle of *non-refoulement* in terms of Art. 3 ECHR, will strengthen the application of this key principle. It could conceivably provide for interesting discussion in, for example, exclusion cases, where member states seek to invoke the exclusion provisions in Art. 17 of the Qualification Directive as grounds for denying subsidiary protection under Art. 15(b). The Charter's unqualified *non-refoulement* obligation would appear to provide a strong argument in favour of protection for individuals who might otherwise be at risk of removal following rejection under Art. 17.

Future of the AFSJ: The Court and asylum

The Lisbon Treaty, with its expanded preliminary reference provisions and legal force for the Charter, has already opened a number of possibilities for the more comprehensive application of international refugee law in European proceedings. Still, there are several future developments or changes that could enhance the tools available to the Court to help it ensure full respect for the rights of those in need of protection.

First, it is hoped that the Court's jurisprudence in preliminary reference cases will draw extensively from refugee protection instruments at the international and regional levels, potentially drawing upon fundamental rights concepts from Community law more generally. The overriding Treaty obligation is for EU asylum instruments to comply with the 1951 Convention. Where EU secondary laws, such as directives or regulations, depart from the wording or object of the 1951 Convention, close scrutiny must be devoted to the issue of how those instruments can be reconciled with this Treaty requirement.

Second, the role of the UNHCR in relation to court proceedings may be a subject for further reflection. Given the UNHCR's supervisory responsibility with respect to the 1951 Convention, it has a direct interest and demonstrated expertise in the application of asylum law in the EU. Its previous inputs to domestic and regional courts as intervenor have demonstrated its ability to contribute constructively to court processes, including in relation to the ECHR, which on several occasions has explicitly invited the UNHCR to intervene in key asylum cases. The present limitation on the UNHCR's ability to intervene before the Court, based on Art. 23 of the Statute, may be something to be addressed in future[33] for the purpose of a more comprehensive and informed legal debate.

Finally, the Stockholm Programme puts forward a proposal that could positively influence the development of the EU's asylum law, including through the courts. The Council in Stockholm stated that subject to a European Commission study, the EU "should seek accession to the 1951 Geneva Convention and its 1967 Protocol".[34] While the Amsterdam and Lisbon Treaties have already affirmed the EU's obligation to respect the 1951 Convention, EU accession would have the benefit of establishing a direct link between the Union institutions and the international protection system, as well as strengthening institutional ties between the UNHCR and the EU. It would be welcomed by other state parties to the Convention as a step that confirms the EU's commitment to refugee protection, and would increase the Union's influence in discussions on the future development of international refugee law and policy. It also has the potential to enhance understanding of and respect for international protection norms throughout the courts of the member states. This could facilitate the Court's task of ensuring compliance with the Convention at all levels of EU action on asylum.

---

[33] There may be alternative ways to achieve this. For instance, the Court may able to take the initiative of calling the UNHCR as an expert witness or otherwise.

[34] Refer to Council of the European Union, The Stockholm Programme – An open and secure Europe serving and protecting the citizens, 17024/09, Brussels, 2 December 2009, p. 69 (retrieved from http://ec.europa.eu/justice_home/fsj/intro/fsj_intro_en.htm).

8. THE MANAGEMENT OF THE EU'S EXTERNAL BORDERS FROM THE CUSTOMS UNION TO FRONTEX AND E-BORDERS

PETER HOBBING

Some history

For an astonishingly long time, matters concerning the external borders of the Union remained in the close neighbourhood of criminal justice and policing within the now-obsolete intergovernmental pillar of the Union. This came as a surprise, especially to those with a more economic vision of the EU, who remembered the common border as part of the Customs Union of 1968 and thus the first flagship achievement of the young Economic Community.[1] But, be it for security or sovereignty concerns as symbolised by traditionally uniformed border guards, no one dared touch this sacred security-oriented concept before the millennium and it was not until 2005 that the change to mainstream policy-making actually occurred.[2]

---

[1] See P. Hobbing, *Integrated Border Management at the EU Level*, CEPS Working Document No. 227, CEPS, Brussels, August 2005, p. 5 (retrieved from http://shop.ceps.eu/BookDetail.php?item_id=1254).

[2] Meanwhile, operational matters even nowadays (!) remain in the intergovernmental niche left under the Lisbon Treaty (Art. 87(2) TFEU).

Yet intergovernmentalism was not the only problem EU border management had to face in its early history. In contrast with individual countries such as the US, which has had a stable territory/borderline for the past 150 years or more, the EU stands out in the changes to its geography, involving new countries, new separation lines and new neighbours. The patchwork process continued after 1999 during the Tampere–Hague phase with ever-increasing speed: 12 new member states plus a few Schengen associates were added – each time entailing new geographical/administrative set-ups as well as inappropriate equipment and staff without adequate experience.[3]

If at the tenth anniversary of the Area of Freedom, Security and Justice (AFSJ) the external border is not considered too problematic a construction site, even less its Achilles' heel, this is owing to a few 'fortunate' if ultimately logical developments. True, the Amsterdam Treaty with its Arts. 62 and 67 had already opened the door halfway to progress, but with sovereignty claims still going strong in national capitals one would not have expected the European Council to take the final decision in favour of the Community method at the earliest possible opportunity.

The Tampere–Hague era

Motors of change were of a mainly pragmatic nature. They included first the 9/11 effect, i.e. the recognition that transnational security threats could no longer be appropriately countered at the national level. And second, there was the (finally economic) argument advanced by the 'heavyweights' Germany and France that a non-operational external border would gradually undermine collective trust, lead to the reintroduction of internal controls and thus jeopardise the entire single market.[4]

---

[3] For details, see P. Hobbing and R. Koslowski, *The Tools Called to Support the 'Delivery' of Freedom, Security and Justice: A Comparison of Border Security Systems in the EU and in the US*, Brussels, PE 410.681, Ad hoc Briefing Note for the LIBE Committee of the European Parliament, February 2009, p.7 ff (retrieved from http://www.ceps.be/system/files/old/ToolsEP.pdf).

[4] See S. Bertozzi, *Schengen: Achievements and Challenges in Managing an Area Encompassing 3.6 million km²*, CEPS Working Document No. 284, CEPS, Brussels, February 2008 (retrieved from http://www.ceps.eu/book/schengenachievements-and-challenges-managing-area-encompassing-36-million-km%C2%B2).

As early as in December 2001, the Laeken European Council positively acknowledged the potential superiority of common management of the external border, by requesting the Council and Commission to devise cooperation arrangements and to examine the conditions in which a mechanism or common service to control external borders could be created. This dictum dealt a final, fatal blow to the absolute sovereignty over national borders as had been recognised as an iron law of statehood ever since the Peace of Westphalia of 1648.

In May 2002, the Commission further stirred up the debate with its Communication on integrated management of the external borders of the member states of the European Union, which culminated in suggesting the possible creation of a "European corps of border guards".[5] The allusion to supranational police forces once again revived old resentments against any Brussels-centred solution - but in the end rejection remained confined to this aspect while backing off on all other issues.

As could be expected, the first generation of 'mechanisms' and 'common services' created with pre-2005 tools (a common manual on checks at the external border and a common unit of external border practitioners) still proved too blunt to ensure coherent protection of the border, while the next stage implemented with Community means of action definitely showed more punch. Frontex, the European Agency for the Management of Operational Cooperation at the External Borders (operational since 2005) and the Community code on the rules governing the movement of persons across borders (the so-called 'Schengen Borders Code' of 2006) thus became reliable cornerstones of the EU's Integrated Border Management (IBM) system. In terms of parallel achievements, one should not overlook the EU framework of border-related IT systems, notably the Schengen Information System II to flag wanted/unwanted persons, the Visa Information System to support the common visa policy and Eurodac to identify asylum seekers on the basis of fingerprints.

The EU's approach in the international context

While (when it comes to external borders) the US and other individual countries may build upon well-founded, monolithic state structures and

[5] Refer to European Commission, Communication, Towards integrated management of the external borders of the member states of the European Union, COM(2002) 233 final, Brussels, 7 May 2002.

quasi-automatically deliver coherent responses, with its patchwork geography the EU still has to struggle hard to come close to such a result. In early 2010, there were 27 states/governments formally responsible for ensuring the protection of their respective segments of the 10,000 kms of land borders, 50,000 kms of sea borders and approximately 1,800 official border-crossing points.

The current formula for resolving this complicated situation consists of the original 2002 elements of i) a common corpus of legislation (the Schengen border code[6] and the Regulation (EC) No. 1931/2006 on local border traffic)[7]; ii) a coordination structure for operational action (Frontex); iii) a burden-sharing arrangement among member states more or less affected by the border (a Schengen facility and EU external borders fund); plus iv) a precise recipe for IBM, notably the need for close cooperation at all levels.[8]

---

[6] See Regulation (EC) No. 562/2006 of the European Parliament and of the Council of 15 March 2006 establishing a Community Code on the rules governing the movement of persons across borders (Schengen Borders Code), OJ L 105/1, 13.4.2006.

[7] See Regulation (EC) No. 1931/2006 of the European Parliament and of the Council of 20 December 2006 laying down rules on local border traffic at the external land borders of the member states and amending the provisions of the Schengen Convention, OJ L 29/3, 3.2.2007.

[8] More specifically, this would include the following aspects:

- border control (checks and surveillance) as defined in the Schengen Borders Code, including relevant risk analysis and crime intelligence;
- detection and investigation of cross-border crime in coordination with all competent law enforcement authorities;
- the four-tier access control model (measures in non-EU countries, cooperation with neighbouring countries, border control, control measures within the area of free movement, including return);
- inter-agency cooperation for border management (border guards, customs, police, national security and other relevant authorities) and international cooperation; and
- coordination and coherence of the activities of member states, institutions and other bodies of the Community and the EU.

If the EU has thus succeeded in filling some crucial gaps in the external borderlines and increasingly takes credit for this in public, it has to do with the following most visible forms of intervention:

- state-of-the-art **upgrades to the technical infrastructure** on the eastern and southern borders (mainly to border-crossing points and naval equipment) thanks to the Schengen facility (€961 million, 2004–06) and the European external borders fund (€1.82 billion foreseen for 2007–13);
- **60+ joint operations** against illegal immigration that have been carried out since 2006, chiefly along the maritime borders, each involving various member states or neighbouring countries and coordinated by Frontex. The interventions around the Canary Islands and southern Italy attracted critical attention for humanitarian reasons. In addition, a permanent maritime, European Patrols Network was set up in 2007;
- the creation of **rapid border intervention teams** (RABITs), based on a pool of border staff (RABITs pool) and equipment (Centralised Records of Available Technical Equipment or CRATE) to help member states at their request in cases of 'exceptional and urgent situations', such as a mass influx of illegal immigrants;
- logistical help for member states, such as **risk analysis strategies** (provided by Frontex); and
- the development of practical **IBM handbooks** as 'export items' for the Western Balkans (under the CARDS programme)[9] and Central Asia (under the BOMCA programme).[10]

Despite remarkable progress notably in the organisational field (Frontex and the IBM strategy), the EU lags behind because of the absence of certain routine features necessary to have full command over the borders. National segments still dominate the picture as a sort of a string of pearls loosely connected. The so-called 'compulsory solidarity' in the event of emergency situations still leaves some escape scenarios for unwilling member states, entry–exit movements across the border are covered by the IT systems in only a fragmentary fashion, and equipment and training

---

[9] CARDS refers to Community Assistance for Reconstruction, Development and Stabilisation.

[10] BOMCA refers to the Border Management Programme for Central Asia.

standards still largely diverge. Similarly, the EU has so far renounced introducing certain forms of air passenger surveillance such as the passenger name record or the electronic system for travel authorisation (ESTA).

Post-2010 outlook

The Commission's border package of February 2008 marked a turning point in EU border strategies: be it through a curious glance over the fence at the US and other partners in the Western world or be it through the assumption that organisational measures had reached their limits, the new trend is clearly characterised by electronic and other technological features ('e-borders').

Quite in contrast to previous years when the European Parliament and Commission fiercely quarrelled with the transatlantic partners over data protection and civil liberties, we now see a striking harmony of concepts. All that seemed of doubtful value before, such as fully automated border checks, comprehensive systems of entry–exit control, air passenger surveillance and electronic travel authorisation, hi-tech border installations including virtual fences, has all of a sudden become part of the EU's vision for the 21st century. In more detail, the threefold package focuses on

- the '**next steps in border management**', i.e. a combination of control and facilitation measures that - psychologically forceful - suggest to the traveller that s/he will gain on both aspects, security and comfort of travel. It includes i) **privileges for 'bona fide' travellers** thanks to biometric identifiers and automated gates; ii) a full-fledged **entry–exit system** allowing the border authorities to determine who is inside and who is outside the territory; and iii) **ESTA**, which following Australian and US models would require passengers to obtain an advance permit before they may board a plane (or possibly other means of transport) to Europe;
- the **future development of Frontex** to allow the agency to obtain more independence in carrying out RABIT/CRATE interventions through the purchase of its own equipment, cooperating with international organisations and non-EU countries. Finally yet importantly, this aspect includes being able to exercise pressure on non-cooperative member states with the hint of the still-available option of a European corps of border guards; and

- a future **European border surveillance system** (EUROSUR) to complement the seamless control at border-crossing points by an equally tight coverage of green/blue borders. Further details have not yet been established but it is understood that first the southern maritime borders are to be secured and later the land borders. Besides interlinking existing national systems, EUROSUR might also include the development of surveillance tools - such as unmanned air vehicles, earth observation technologies, border-related intelligence processes and a US-style 'virtual fence'.

Reactions were mixed, with applause for the improved organisational role of Frontex, yet with considerable doubts regarding the vast **technological build-up** proposed: it is true that the threats and challenges have become more complex, but technology does not present solutions for everything.

There may be frustration about the slow progress in handling the border in a cooperative manner among the member states concerned, whereby technology is seen as a neutral way to ensure secure surveillance without the presence of 'foreign' staff on national territory. Technology also seems to offer tempting formulas to reconcile the permanent conflict between security and travel facilitation: the more you rely on automation/IT, the more you can reduce waiting queues at airports while making no concessions on maximum security standards. And finally there is an interesting promotional aspect for European industry: if Europe seeks to catch up with overseas competitors in security research by means of the €1.4 billion European Security Research Programme, why not take advantage of opportunities that open up right on the doorstep?

While all this underpins the argument for more technology in border management, the majority of comments remain rather sceptical towards the breathtaking advance of hi-tech equipment and the mass processing of personal data in the form of a 'digital tsunami'.[11] Not only does such collection and processing of data represent per se a far-reaching intrusion into privacy, but also quantity matters. The more data there is in the transfer patterns and profiling systems employed, the greater the risk of

---

[11] Refer to E. Guild and S. Carrera, *Towards the Next Phase of the EU's Area of Freedom, Security and Justice: The European Commission's Proposals for the Stockholm Programme*, CEPS Policy Brief No. 196, CEPS, Brussels, August 2009, p. 7 (available from http://shop.ceps.be/downfree.php?item_id=1899).

data leakage, erroneous results and painful consequences for the individuals concerned. The European data protection authorities constantly point to these risks.

Likewise, we know from long-term US experience - as the world's most authentic 'testing laboratory' for border security - that even enormous investments in advanced technology have not been able to render America's borders watertight. Owing to the remaining loopholes and despite virtual and other fences, the famous entry–exit system is still not fully operational. US government experts openly recognise these difficulties, but curiously enough, over here no one seems to be taking note.

To avoid any misunderstanding, this is not to discredit technical progress as such; but as with all long-term policy-making, such landmark decisions require profound reasoning and consideration. Fortunately, the EU has established formal procedures to prepare such decisions with sufficient care. Most of all, the Lisbon Treaty, with the full involvement of the European Parliament, should now ensure transparent discussions and due consideration of expertise, especially in data protection matters. In addition, discussions should not remain limited to issues of legal or ethical compatibility - in many instances problems start in the practical field. 'Is the proposed concept likely to work?' should be the first question.[12]

Expensive strategies are not likely to produce a clear added value - e.g. an entry–exit system along the lines of the non-operational US model would not only mean a waste of public money but also violate the general principle of **proportionality**. Equally, IT systems that are not necessary as their purpose is already covered by existing instruments would be illegal, as they infringe the standard data protection criterion of suitability/proportionality.[13]

---

[12] See D. Bigo and J. Jeandesboz, *Border Security, Technology and the Stockholm Programme*, INEX Policy Brief No. 3, November 2009, p. 3 (retrieved from http://www.ceps.be/book/border-security-technology-and-stockholm-programme).

[13] Refer to Hobbing and Koslowski (2009), op. cit., p. 27.

Conclusions

In conclusion, it is suggested that future border strategies should avoid a unilateral emphasis on technical solutions but pursue other promising and less risky tracks.

One such measure could be the revision of the Schengen evaluation mechanism in the sense of more frequent and unannounced control visits:[14] less intergovernmentalism and more 'federal' responsibility would be the right signal to achieve a homogeneous implementation of the Schengen border code and thus a more coherent and secure border. Without monumental investments in border infrastructure or data systems, promising results may be obtained in numerous other ways, e.g. by taking advantage of the existing second-line controls in the workplace.[15]

As a lesson to be retained for the forthcoming consolidation period of the AFSJ it seems most important that mutual trust among the member states (as well as between them and the institutions) represents the most precious element for the *bon fonctionnement* of the external border. Technology can replace this only to a limited degree. Despite all the difficulties and partial glitches, Frontex has managed to accumulate a considerable amount of confidence and goodwill among national authorities, to the extent that RABITs operations and other interventions from the central level are no longer met with suspicion, as was the case a couple of years ago. It may just be a small token of change, but a newspaper headline from somewhere in the north-eastern outskirts of Schengenland, "Foreign uniforms can now guard borders [with] Russia", indicates a certain degree of normality. Such a change contrasts with 1999, yet appears even more remarkable if one remembers the TREVI[16] times of

---

[14] As currently proposed by European Commission, Proposal for a Council Regulation on the establishment of an evaluation mechanism to verify the application of the Schengen acquis proposal COM(2009) 102 final, Brussels, 4 March 2009.

[15] See Hobbing and Koslowski (2009), op. cit., p. 12.

[16] The intergovernmental working group TREVI (*Terrorisme, radicalisme, extremisme et violence internationale*) created in 1975 as a reaction against expanding Euro-terrorism (the RAF, Brigate Rosse), represented the first attempt to counter security threats through EU-wide cooperation. TREVI is seen as the forerunner of the third pillar under the Maastricht Treaty of 1992, whose new organisational structures gradually absorbed TREVI and its various sub-groups in the early 1990s.

the early 1990s when mutual trust was so low that Commission representatives had to leave the meeting room during "sensitive" discussions.[17]

Recommendations

The following recommendations are made in light of the above considerations:

1) The external borders require a high degree of efficiency and legitimacy, which can only be accomplished through a full communitarisation/Europeanisation of its management. Intergovernmental elements should be eliminated where still found, notably by an overhaul of the Frontex regulation. The exemption still granted to operational action should come under close scrutiny.
2) Rather than indiscriminately copying foreign models, the EU should carefully examine their appropriateness and adequacy for the European situation, which includes above all the testing of their practical efficiency. Systems unfit at home, such as the US entry-exit system, are not likely to work in Europe either.
3) The borders, as high-risk spots for human rights-related offences ranging from privacy to refugee rights, require appropriate mechanisms of democratic control, possibly in the form of a border monitor.
4) Frontex needs to redefine its IBM concept to include free movement, trade and customs aspects, and thus demonstrate the end of a unilateral focus on security.

Technology has shown its limits elsewhere. One should not overestimate its benefits for the European context. Before investing in expensive new projects, one should first a) request evidence supporting the need for and efficiency of the systems proposed; and b) examine alternative mechanisms (e.g. second-line inland controls, revised Schengen evaluation rules, and greater independence of Frontex in logistical and staffing terms) for the extent to which they are likely to produce the same or even better results.

---

[17] As recalled by Adrian Fortescue, first director-general of the Directorate-General for Justice and Home Affairs (1999-2003), in a speech given at the Bundeskriminalamt in Wiesbaden in November 1999.

9. JUDICIAL COOPERATION IN THE EU EUROJUST AND THE EUROPEAN PUBLIC PROSECUTOR

HANS G. NILSSON

The creation of Eurojust has always been intimately connected to the idea of the creation of a European public prosecutor (EPP),[1] although it is probably true to say that Eurojust, as a judicial cooperation tool, had been in the minds of some persons since the beginning of the 1990s. This was a reaction to Chancellor Helmut Kohl's ideas of Europol becoming a 'European FBI'.

In the middle of that decade, ideas on the creation of a European public prosecutor also began to take root, in particular in the context of the protection of the financial interests of the Community, where the Directorate-General for Budget at the Commission was a driving force. In the same context, magistrates in Europe began to protest against the way that mutual legal assistance was handled by political authorities, the most famous expression being the '*Appel de Génève*'.[2]

[1] See H.G. Nilsson, "Eurojust: The Beginning or the End of the European Public Prosecutor?", *Europarättslig Tidskrift*, Vol. 3, No. 4, 2000. For a general discussion of the EPP, see E. Ramos and V. Carbajosa (eds), *The Future European Public Prosecutor's Office*, Madrid: Imprenta Nacional del Boletin Oficial del Estado, 2009.

[2] See D. Robert, *La Justice ou le Chaos*, Paris: Stock, 1996.

But as with nearly all European projects, the idea of the EPP was way before its time - it had been forgotten that Europe practically never creates anything as a Big Bang - it has always been step by step, through practical cooperation and the advancement of ideas, through pilot projects and trial and error.

Nevertheless, if one had said ten years ago that Eurojust would exist, that it would coordinate more than 1,000 cases per year and organise more than 100 coordination meetings, that it would coordinate serious and organised crime cases and terrorist investigations, most policy-makers, experts, professors - and also prosecutors - would have considered this unthinkable. Yet Eurojust exists, and it does precisely that. And it does it with success, as the growing confidence in the young unit shows.

If one would have said ten years ago that the EPP or at least the possibility of it would now become a practical possibility and inserted into the Treaty of Lisbon, that also would have been unthinkable for most except the most optimistic (or unrealistic).[3] Today, the fact is that the EPP is now in Art. 86 of the Treaty and that it is suddenly no longer utopia. Already this should be considered a great step. Even so, we are not there yet. And it would be wrong to think that it will be an easy path towards its establishment. On the contrary, and unless something dramatic occurs, it will still take several years, if not decades before we are there. Several steps will have to be fulfilled, each of them fraught with difficulties and delicate choices.

What are the probable steps that will have to happen in the future before we will come to the stage of the European public prosecutor? The following is in my opinion the possible scenario for the future.

First, the Eurojust Decision (2002/187/JHA)[4] was recently amended through a Council Decision (2009/426/JHA)[5] that brought the

---

[3] In 1999, I noted that "people who started to speak about the European Monetary Union perhaps 20 or 40 years ago were at a similar stage as [those who] started the Corpus Juris project" (see H.G. Nilsson, in B. Huber (ed.), *Das Corpus Juris als Grundlage eines Europäischen Strafrechts*, Freiburg: Edition Iuscrim, 2000).

[4] See Council of the European Union, Decision 2002/187/JHA of 28 February 2002 setting up Eurojust with a view to reinforcing the fight against serious crime, OJ L 63/1, 6.3.2002.

organisational structure, the handing-in of information to Eurojust, the tasks (read 'powers') and abilities to render the work more efficient more in line with the experiences so far in European judicial cooperation. A national coordination system was set up, thereby closing the gap between The Hague and capitals, linking capitals and judicial authorities with the case management system of Eurojust and creating real possibilities for seeing links between cases that could not be seen before. The obligation on member states to send information automatically in the most serious cases was considerably augmented and the organisational stability of Eurojust was strengthened so that it would not become a victim of national whims and uncertainties. Eurojust's ability to work together with partners and non-EU countries was also strengthened, for instance by giving it the possibility to send liaison magistrates to non-EU countries. The College of Eurojust was additionally given the possibility to issue non-binding opinions in certain respects, such as when conflicts of jurisdiction arise.

It seems clear that after this rather substantive overhaul of the Eurojust organisational set-up most member states would not be prepared to go into discussions on an EPP at this stage. They would rather be prepared to let Eurojust consolidate itself, implement the new provisions and let the national coordination systems settle themselves and find their role at the national and international levels.

Second, after some time has elapsed (probably five years), member states would probably believe that it would be time to evaluate the impact and efficiency of the Decision. After such an evaluation, one could possibly consider whether changes could be made with a view to rendering the Eurojust set-up more efficient.

The Lisbon Treaty points in two different directions, compared with the Amsterdam Treaty.

Art. 85(1)(a) mentions as a "task" of Eurojust "the initiation of criminal investigations", while at the same time Art. 85(2) indicates that "formal acts of judicial procedure shall be carried out by the competent national officials".[6] The question here is what is meant by "initiation"? The

---

[5] See Council of the European Union, Decision 2009/426/JHA of 16 December 2008 on the strengthening of Eurojust and amending Decision 2002/187/JHA, OJ L 138/14, 4.6.2009.

[6] Refer to the Treaty on the Functioning of the European Union ('Lisbon Treaty'), Consolidated version, OJ C 115/47, 9.5.2008.

term is not used in the Amsterdam Treaty, as amended by the Nice Treaty. As Eurojust already existed when the Nice Treaty entered into force, it should mean something more than what was already on the table. Eurojust, acting either through a national member or through the College, already had the 'power' to ask a national authority to initiate a criminal investigation. Therefore, the conclusion that I come to is that the task of "initiation" must mean that a national authority has an *obligation* to initiate the investigation in accordance with national law. Clearly, that will be a revolution in judicial circles in several member states, at least if this power is given to the College of Eurojust and not only to a national member. In the negotiations on the recent Eurojust Decision a number of member states even had constitutional difficulties in accepting that their own national members could act independently. It was as if the move to The Hague deprived them from all the judicial powers they had in their home countries.

The other direction in which the Lisbon Treaty opens up further possibilities is in the "resolution" of conflicts of jurisdiction (see Art. 85(1)(c)). This term did not figure in the Nice Treaty[7] either, so it must mean something more and different from what Eurojust can do now. Is a written, non-binding opinion in a case enough? In my opinion it cannot be, given that if the national authorities do not agree or if their opinions differ, it would seem that no "resolution" has been found and a Eurojust "task" cannot be fulfilled. Therefore, it would appear that there is no other possibility than to make opinions from Eurojust (at least when acting as a College) mandatory for national authorities. Evidently, this would also be a revolution in many member states and may well (like the previous point) necessitate constitutional amendments in the member states.

Third, I believe that we will have to make a real impact assessment, not only evaluating the functioning of Eurojust, but also particularly whether there is **a need** for an EPP in the light of how Eurojust works and how judicial cooperation in the protection of the financial interests of the Union works. Member states will not, at the present stage, be prepared to go through with what will be extremely complex and no doubt very lengthy discussions that will be required before an EPP can start to function, unless a real need has been demonstrated in an unambiguous manner.

---

[7] The Nice Treaty instituted Eurojust into the Treaties.

Therefore, the paradox is that the more successful Eurojust is, the less there will be a need for a European public prosecutor. And there is a double paradox: for the member states that do not want an EPP, they would have an interest in prioritising Eurojust as much as possible, which may include giving judicial powers to their national member in accordance with Art. 9 of the Eurojust Decision, for instance in all urgent cases or in relation to the joint investigation teams. Those member states that will support the EPP should also be able to support giving further powers to Eurojust, because this goes in the right direction for them, namely towards creating a European public prosecutor. Moreover, the success of Eurojust is also an objective shared by *all* member states.

If we assume that the EPP will be set up, the two bodies will have to work side by side. How exactly that will be done will be a matter for the future, and it will not become one of the easier issues to discuss, but I would like to give some indications of own thoughts on the subject.

As the Lisbon Treaty requires unanimity to establish the EPP, it seems clear that this will not be achievable in the near future if one were to aim at this option. Therefore, the only other option would appear to be to create the EPP through enhanced cooperation in accordance with the provisions of Art. 20 TEU and Arts. 326-334 TFEU, which would require that at least nine member states would be prepared, as a last resort, to set up the EPP (and subjugate themselves to its powers).

It should be emphasised that the enhanced cooperation may only concern the EPP for the protection of the financial interests of the Union. The way the Lisbon Treaty is currently drafted would seem to mean that enhanced cooperation here cannot be adopted for the purpose of, for example, fighting organised crime or terrorism, unless the Council, after obtaining the consent of the European Parliament and after consulting the Commission, unanimously decides to add competences (see Art. 86, para. 4).

But this is only the beginning of the trials and tribulations for the nine member states that are willing to take this step.

Setting aside any changes to their own constitutions (and it is highly likely that nearly all member states will have to do that) and the complicated procedures to achieve enhanced cooperation, the member states will also have to agree (according to Art. 86, para. 3) on the

- general rules applicable to the EPP's office,
- conditions governing the performance of its functions,
- rules of procedure applicable to its activities,

- rules of procedure governing the admissibility of evidence, and
- rules applicable to the judicial review of procedural measures taken by the EPP in the performance of its functions.

Given the diversified nature of the codes of criminal procedure of all member states, also as regards those that originally adopted the Napoleonic Code, this seems to be a mammoth task. One needs only to think of the differences in our judicial institutions, the role of the prosecutor in the member states, the diverse functions and powers of investigating judges, and the various methods of organisation of the courts. These judicial institutions all have different powers and functions in the member states. Moreover, the issue of judicial review of the EPP will no doubt turn out to be difficult, and if one foresees using the Court of Justice for such a review, this may require a Treaty change.

As the EPP, at least in the beginning, will be limited to the protection of the financial interests of the Union, Eurojust will remain in its present - or possibly changed - structure. The question then is following: How will the two bodies function together?

The Lisbon Treaty provides that the EPP will be created *from* Eurojust (Art. 86, para. 1). What does this mean in reality?

Many different solutions could be considered. The EPP could become a kind of 28th national member of Eurojust and sit in the College every time the protection of the financial interests of the Union is discussed. Only those national members of Eurojust representing the nine member states would be present. Another alternative would be that it is the College of Eurojust *itself* that would become the EPP, and within the national offices of Eurojust (current National Coordination System), one could in such a scenario also find the deputy EPP, who would represent the EPP at the national level. This could possibly be a national member or a deputy to a national member of Eurojust. Yet only time will tell if this is realistic.

10. POLICE COOPERATION ON AN EU-WIDE LEVEL 1998–2010

DEVELOPMENTS AND CHALLENGES

JOHANNES VOS

Introduction

It is a challenging task to explain in 3,000 words the successes and failures of police cooperation in the last ten years and the challenges in light of the Lisbon Treaty. My conclusion is that the successes are in a way remarkable (the creation of Europol and the adoption of the Prüm framework), while there are what could be qualified as deficiencies rather than failures (the start-up phase of Europol and the European Police College (CEPOL), implementation of the availability principle, and a lack of balance between security and data protection). The challenges ahead are in the areas of data protection, the better functioning of agencies, the role of different organs in the implementation of the internal security strategy, and the way the Commission and European Parliament assume new tasks and responsibilities.

Police cooperation 1998–2008

Bases

Police cooperation started in 1975 under the TREVI framework, with special attention given to cooperation against terrorism. The Maastricht Treaty that entered into force on 1 November 1993 defined police cooperation, including the creation of Europol as a matter of common interest. Police cooperation was brought into the remit of the European Union. Decision-making was basically intergovernmental.

The Amsterdam Treaty, which was signed on 2 October 1997 and entered into force on 1 May 1999, contained more precise provisions on police cooperation. It extended the right of proposal to the Commission. Legal acts can take the form of common positions, framework decisions, decisions and conventions.

The Schengen *acquis* was integrated into the framework of the European Union.

During the period under review, work was also based on the Viennese action plan[1] (adopted in December 1998), the conclusions of the Tampere European Council[2] (15-16 October 1999) and The Hague Programme[3] (adopted on 4-5 November 2004).

The Viennese action plan focused on the development of Europol and the Convention that entered into force on 1 January 1999. Other measures were also mentioned, such as arrangements under which a law-enforcement service from one member state could operate in the territory of another, and the development and expansion of operational cooperation.

In the Tampere conclusions, besides the regular reference to Europol as a critical body to combat crime, the creation of a European chiefs task force and a European police college were foreseen.

The impact of the 9/11 events was widely reflected in The Hague Programme. Strengthening security was an important element. Improving the exchange of information became a priority (the availability principle): throughout the Union a law enforcement officer in one member state who needed information to perform his/her duties was to be able to obtain this from another member state. The law enforcement agency in the other member state holding this information was to make it available for the

---

[1] Refer to the Action Plan of the Council and the Commission on how best to implement the provisions of the Treaty of Amsterdam on an Area of Freedom, Security and Justice, Text adopted by the Justice and Home Affairs Council on 3 December 1998, OJ C 19/1, 23.1.1999.

[2] See European Council, Presidency Conclusions of the Tampere European Council of 15-16 October, SN 200/1/99, Brussels, 1999.

[3] See European Council, Presidency Conclusions of the Brussels European Council of 4-5 November, SN 14292/04, Annex I, 5 December 2004.

stated purpose, taking into account the requirement of ongoing investigations in that state.

Police forces were invited to contribute to actions against the financing of terrorism, as well as actions against radicalisation and recruitment. Improving the security of the storage and transport of explosives as well as ensuring the traceability of industrial and chemical precursors were also recommended.

Furthermore, the role of Europol was stressed, with more use to be made of joint investigative teams. Police cooperation among member states was to focus on specific themes and special areas (cross-border).

Achievements

Looking over the entire 1998–2008 period and taking into account the various aforementioned commitments, it is correct to say that many, if not most, of the tasks have been implemented.

This may sound self-evident, but prominent theorists of international relations arguing that integration can only proceed primarily in sectors not at the core of the nation-state and with a key role for an institution such as the Commission might have problems explaining the creation of Europol in particular.

Europol

Europol has played an important role in police cooperation at the EU level. Its creation was suggested at the European Council in June 1991 in Luxembourg by the German Chancellor Helmut Kohl.

Experts are not yet sure whether his initiative was driven by a need to show his European commitment after the fall of the Berlin Wall or by a fear of rising international crime. Possibly both factors may have played a part.

The Europol Convention[4] entered into force in January 1999. Its mandate, originally limited to unlawful drug trafficking, trafficking in nuclear and radioactive substances, illegal immigrant smuggling, trafficking in human beings and motor vehicle crime, was progressively extended to cover all major forms of crime, including terrorism.

---

[4] See the Convention based on Article K.3 of the Treaty on European Union, on the establishment of a European Police Office ('Europol Convention'), OJ C 316/2, 27.12.1995.

Protocols adopted in November 2002[5] and November 2003[6] defined Europol's involvement in joint investigation teams, strengthened Europol's operational support function with respect to national police authorities and emphasised the important functions of Europol in the field of cross-border crime, investigation in support of Union-wide crime prevention, analysis and investigation.

Prüm

A major step forward in cross-border cooperation was the Treaty between Belgium, Germany, Spain, France, Luxembourg, the Netherlands and Austria on the stepping up of the fight against cross-border crime and illegal migration signed in Prüm on 27 May 2005.

In consultation with the European Commission, the substance of the provisions of this Treaty was submitted to the Council with the aim of incorporating them in the legal framework of the European Union. A previous text proposed by the Commission covering similar matters as those in the Prüm Treaty could not be agreed in the Council.

The January–June 2007 German presidency played a crucial role in presenting and advancing work in the Council. The final Decision (2008/615/JHA) and an implementing text (2008/616/JHA) were adopted on 23 June 2008.[7] [8]

The objective of the Decision is to improve the exchange of information, whereby member states grant one another access rights to

---

[5] See the Protocol amending the Convention on the establishment of a European Police Office (Europol Convention) and the Protocol on the privileges and immunities of Europol, the members of its organs, the deputy directors and the employees of Europol, OJ C 312/2, 16.12.2002.

[6] See the Protocol Drawn up on the basis of Article 43(1) of the Convention on the Establishment of a European Police Office (Europol Convention), amending that Convention, OJ C 2/3, 6.1.2004.

[7] See Council of the European Union, Council Decision 2008/615/JHA of 23 June 2008 on the stepping up of cross-border cooperation, particularly in combating terrorism and cross-border crime, OJ L 210/1, 6.8.2008.

[8] See Council of the European Union, Council Decision 2008/616/JHA of 23 June 2008 on the implementation of Decision 2008/615/JHA on the stepping up of cross-border cooperation, particularly in combating terrorism and cross-border crime, OJ L 210/12, 6.8. 2008.

their automated DNA analysis files, automated dactyloscopic identification systems and vehicle registration data. The principle of availability should be applied. Cross-border data comparison should open up a new dimension in fighting crime, resulting in new investigative approaches for member states. The text also contains provisions for the supply of data in connection with major events with a cross-border dimension and the prevention of terrorist offences. Joint operations of designated officials in the context of maintaining public order and security and preventing criminal offences are also covered in the Decision.

The Decision is a text with a wide scope, creating a central framework for operational police cooperation. More than in previous texts, attention is paid to data protection. As regards the processing of personal data, each member state shall at least guarantee a level of protection equal to that resulting from the pertinent Council of Europe texts of January 1981 and September 1987.

CEPOL

Pursuant to the conclusions of the European Council of Tampere of 1999, CEPOL was created in December 2000.[9] It is a network bringing together national training institutes for senior police officers. CEPOL has its seat in Bramshill, UK.

Among its main objectives are to increase knowledge of the national police systems and structures of other member states, of Europol and of cross-border police cooperation within the European Union; it also seeks to strengthen knowledge of international instruments, in particular those already existing at the European Union level in the field of cooperation on combating crime.

Task Force of European Police Chiefs

Pursuant to the conclusions of the Tampere European Council, a Task Force of the Chiefs of Police was established in 2000. It meets twice a year on a strategic level and also twice a year on a more operational level. It deals at a strategic level with more general issues not fully covered by other bodies.

[9] See the Initiative of the Portuguese Republic with a view to the adoption of a Council Decision on the provisional establishment of the European Police College, OJ C 206/3, 19.7.2000.

At the operational level, special attention is paid to projects under the initiative for Comprehensive, Operational, Strategic Planning for the Police (COSPOL), in which a group of member states in conjunction with the participation of Europol draws up an operational project in certain fields (e.g. synthetic drugs, cocaine and the trafficking of human beings) under the aegis of a lead country.

Other matters

Since 1998, the Council has adopted soft law (i.e. resolutions and conclusions) on the protection of public figures and security at football games. Council bodies have additionally dealt with relations with the Union, especially Europol and the South-East European Cooperation Initiative.

Cooperation between EU police forces and Europol, for example in Kosovo as regards data collection and analysis of organised crime, has also drawn the attention of the Council.

Assessment

Looking at the commitments in the Maastricht and Amsterdam Treaties along with the Vienna, Tampere and Hague action plans/programmes, it can be concluded that to a large extent missions have been accomplished. All the frameworks are in place: Europol, CEPOL and the Prüm Decision.

Insufficiencies in the decision-making process that have been stressed regularly (unanimity and the lack of European Parliament involvement) do not seem to have hampered progress. A well-planned, well-coordinated initiative of a key delegation can have a decisive impact.

This was the case in July 1994 as regards the Europol Convention and in January 2007 with respect to the Prüm Decision. Both initiatives were presented and successfully carried forward by the German ministry of interior in the context of the German presidency.

Agencies such as Europol and CEPOL have had starting problems. In this respect, the delay in the full operational phase of the Europol Information System was regrettable. More and more cases are being initiated by Europol (from 1,919 in 2000 to 8,377 in 2008).

Europol has a major role in the drawing up the Organised Crime Threat Assessment report (OCTA and ROCTA on Russia). Its budget rose from €28 million in 2000 to €64 million in 2008. There were 622 persons working for Europol in December 2008. On 31 December 2008, operational agreements were in place with seven countries, Eurojust and Interpol. Strategic agreements were in place with seven countries and eight organisations.

It is too early to assess the implementation of the Prüm Decision.

The Task Force of the Chiefs of Police has been looking for its role apart from Europol and Council structures. COSPOL projects were not always successful and the meetings at strategic level were ever less attended by the heads of police.

Over the course of time, increasing attention - although not enough according to many observers - has been paid to data protection.

Looking back, the 1998–2008 period may have been a crucial stage in EU-wide police cooperation. Important instruments and bodies were put in place. It was the creative phase.

Lisbon Treaty/Stockholm Programme

Lisbon Treaty[10]

In establishing a space of freedom, justice and security, the Commission and European Parliament saw their roles expanded by the Lisbon Treaty.

A shared right of proposal for the Commission, qualified majority and co-decision by the European Parliament applies to the following areas:

- the collection, storage, processing/analysis and exchange of relevant information;
- support for training and cooperation on the exchange of staff, on equipment and on research into crime detection; and
- common investigative techniques in relation to the detection of serious forms of organised crime. Operational cooperation will be decided by the Council unanimously after consultation with the European Parliament. A special procedure is foreseen for strengthened cooperation among a limited number of member states.

  Only a quarter of the member states have the right of initiative.

[10] See the Treaty on the Functioning of the European Union ('Lisbon Treaty'), Consolidated version, OJ C 115/47, 9.5.2008.

A single article (Art. 88) is devoted to Europol. Its provisions have already been largely incorporated in the Council decision establishing the European Police Office. That was adopted in 2008 and will apply from 1 January 2010.[11] Europol will be an entity of the European Union, funded from the general budget of the European Communities. The responsibilities of the European Parliament in the control of Europol will be enhanced.

Europol can now assist the competent authorities, the member states, without the limitation that there must be factual indication that an organised criminal structure is involved. Participation in joint investigative teams is being facilitated. The position of a data protection officer has been created.

The Lisbon Treaty itself provides that through the co-decision procedure, the operation, fields of action and tasks of Europol shall be agreed. The same procedure applies to control of Europol by the European Parliament and national parliaments.

Stockholm Programme[12]

As The Hague Programme came to its term and with the entry into force of the Lisbon Treaty being imminent, at its meeting of December 2009 the European Council adopted the Stockholm Programme, with the subheading "An open and secure Europe serving and protecting the citizens".

The major focus of this programme is migration/asylum. As regards police cooperation, reference is made to the definition of a comprehensive, internal security strategy.

Among its principles are stringent cooperation among EU agencies, including further improving information exchange and the use of regional initiatives and regional cooperation.

---

[11] See Council of the European Union, Proposal for a Council Decision establishing the European Police Office (Europol) - Consolidated text, 8296/08, Brussels, 10 April 2008.

[12] See Council of the European Union, The Stockholm Programme - An open and secure Europe serving and protecting the citizens, 17024/09, Brussels, 2 December 2009.

The Internal Security Committee, set up under Art. 71 of the Lisbon Treaty to promote and strengthen operational cooperation, is tasked with monitoring, developing and implementing the internal security strategy.

Managing the flow of information with particular attention to an appropriate data protection regime is a priority. The forthcoming information strategy should be driven by law enforcement needs and aim at the interoperability of IT systems.

The key role of Europol is confirmed providing that it should become a hub for information exchange among the law enforcement authorities of the member states, a service provider and a platform for law enforcement services. Joint investigative teams should be used more often as a tool. Europol has to work more closely with the police missions that take place under the European security and defence policy.

Moreover, the Commission, and where appropriate the Council and high representative, are invited to

- examine how Europol's receipt of information from member states could be ensured and how operational cooperation could be stepped up, e.g. as regards the incompatibility of information systems and other equipment, and the use of undercover agents;
- consider developing a police cooperation code for consolidating existing instruments, and where necessary amend and simplify them; and
- promote operational agreements among the EU agencies and their participation in regional initiatives.

Pilot projects in cross-border regional cooperation such as the Joint Police and Customs Centres should be promoted.

Follow-up

In the light of and pursuant to the adoption of the Lisbon Treaty/Stockholm Programme, various initiatives have been developed. A proposal for an information management strategy for EU internal security was adopted in December 2009. An internal security strategy was agreed by the Council in February 2010.[13] The Standing Committee on Internal

[13] See Council of the European Union, Draft Internal Security Strategy for the European Union: 'Towards a European Security Model', 5842/2/10, Brussels, 23 February 2010.

Security (COSI) had its first meeting on 11 March 2010. In addition, a JHA trio-presidency programme was presented on 4 January 2010[14] reflecting the commitments of the Stockholm Programme.

Challenges

Looking back over the last ten years, it is nearly impossible to speak about failures. There have been insufficiencies that have been coped with (e.g. through new Europol texts and the Prüm Decision). Institutional flexibility, considered by some a weakness, may have been behind some major successes (e.g. advanced under the German presidencies in 1994 and 2007). The provision that a quarter of the member states can present an initiative should be assessed in a positive way.

- An absolute necessity now is to strike a better balance between security and data protection concerns in view of the reservations expressed by the European Parliament and civil society. Over time, in pertinent texts - such as The Hague action plan, Stockholm Programme, Prüm Decision and the decision on Europol - increasing attention is being paid to data protection. It should be a priority for the Commission, as stated in the Stockholm Programme, to evaluate the functioning of the various instruments on data protection and where necessary, to present further legislative and non-legislative initiatives. The three presidencies have already ensured indispensable modifications to the Framework Decision (2008/977/JHA) on the protection of personal data processed in the framework of police and judicial cooperation in criminal matters.[15] On a practical level, a representation of EU data protection authorities could be invited to attend COSI meetings.
- On an institutional level, the roles of the European Commission and Parliament have increased. The European Parliament has a right of co-decision on most legislative matters except on measures covering operational cooperation on which it is consulted. National

---

[14] Council of the European Union, JHA Trio Presidency Programme (January 2010 - June 2011), 5008/10, Brussels, 2 February 2010.

[15] See Council of the European Union, Council Framework Decision 2008/977/JHA of 27 November 2008 on the protection of personal data processed in the framework of police and judicial cooperation in criminal matters, OJ L 350/60, 30.12.2008.

parliaments also are part of the decision-making process, e.g. as regards Europol. The Commission has been invited to present an action plan pursuant to the Stockholm Programme as well as a communication on the European security strategy. It is essential that the Commission, Council trio presidencies, European Parliament and Council Secretariat organise their collaboration (who, what and when). In this regard, the European Parliament could ask that it is also more involved in the drawing-up of programmes, strategies, action plans, and where possible, soft legislation. In view of the new competences of the European Parliament, the relationship between the European Parliament and Europol should be defined.

- Operational cooperation has to be promoted and organised. The various agencies (Europol, Eurojust, Frontex, the European Anti-Fraud Office and CEPOL) will have to coordinate their activities. Regional initiatives (e.g. the Baltic Sea Task Force, Salzburg Forum, Drugs Intelligence Centres in Lisbon and Toulon, and the Joint Police and Customs Centre in Luxembourg) have to be developed. The COSI has to steer this work and give the needed impulses. Better use should also be made of joint investigative teams.

After the period of creativity (1995–2008) in police cooperation, it is now time for enhancing implementation of the existing instruments and improving the functioning of existing organisations. In this respect, the roles of the Chiefs of Police Task Force and CEPOL deserve special attention. The Chiefs of Police Task Force could be absorbed by COSI and CEPOL, or could become a part of Europol in the new phase of police cooperation, where coordination, streamlining, and the most efficient application of complex procedures and data protection should be priorities.

Finally, in order to allow for some introspection and criticism, regular annual contact between decision-makers and leading academics could be very useful.

11. THE EXTERNAL DIMENSION OF THE FIGHT AGAINST TERRORISM
EXTERNAL AND INTERNAL SECURITY

KARL VON WOGAU

As a first reaction after the terrorist attacks against the twin towers in Manhattan, US President George W. Bush declared a "war against terrorism". And it is true that some of the preparations had taken place in countries outside the US. In a world of global communications and transport it is not possible to draw a clear line between the internal and the external aspects of security. This is a basic fact we have to take into account when reflecting on homeland security in the European Union.

The training camps of al-Qaeda are an important element of the threat coming from abroad. One of the reasons given in Germany for our engagement in Afghanistan is that Hindelang in Bavaria has to be defended in the mountains of the Hindu Kush. Meanwhile, the camps in Afghanistan have been destroyed, but we find them again in Pakistan, Yemen and Sub-Saharan Africa.

Border controls are not a negligible element of homeland security in the US. Anyone who has made a trip to the US in recent years will confirm this point. In Europe, we have common external borders for goods, services and capital, and other external borders of the countries that belong to the Schengen area. This does not facilitate an efficient supervision of these borders.

Efficient controls at the borders are very much dependent upon close cooperation among the authorities on both sides. At best, customs control and border police should be housed in the same buildings to facilitate formal and informal exchanges of information. That is one of the reasons our European Neighbourhood Policy can be an important part of the security policy of the European Union.

Another aspect of the external dimension of our security policy is the solidarity clause of the Treaty of Lisbon. It says that the Union and its member states shall act jointly in a spirit of solidarity if a member state is the object of a terrorist attack or subject to a natural or manmade disaster.[1] The Treaty affirms that in such a case the Union shall mobilise all the instruments at its disposal, including the military resources made available by the member states.

Is Europe a target for terrorists?

Citizens of the European Union have a tendency to consider terrorism a threat that mainly concerns the US. They do not take into account that Islamic terrorism has clearly declared Europe as one of its targets. They forget the terrorist attacks in London and Madrid and the failed attacks in Germany. Additionally, we have to be aware of the number of European participants in terrorist training camps all over the world.

We also have to take into consideration that the objectives of terrorism have changed. Andreas Baader, Ulrike Meinhof and the Brigate Rosse had representatives of the state and industry as their targets. What they were looking for was what the Italians call *cadaveri illustri*. This has profoundly changed. Today's terrorism threatens every citizen of our countries.

The most worrying threat is the combination of terrorism and weapons of mass destruction. As a warning from bioterrorism, we have seen the Aum sect in Japan using sarin and anthrax. Nuclear terrorism would be even more disastrous. Nuclear weapons in the hands of failed or irresponsible states would be a terrible threat. For the purpose of terrorism, they do not even need the full technology of missiles and enrichment. The use of what is called a 'dirty bomb' would be sufficient.

I remember a simulation of such a terrorist event that was run for the Subcommittee for Security and Defence of the European Parliament. The

---

[1] See Art. 222 of the Treaty on the Functioning of the European Union ('Lisbon Treaty'), Consolidated version, OJ C 115/47, 9.5.2008.

scenario was that the necessary material for a dirty bomb was smuggled into the territory of the European Union from an eastern country. The bomb was exploded in the vicinity of Brussels airport and we were confronted with a nuclear cloud moving across the Benelux countries in the direction of Germany.

Just try to imagine the situation of the European Union and the member states when confronted with aggression of this kind. Nuclear material can be found mainly in territories where the supervision of the state does not function properly. This is one of the reasons the European security strategy considers failed states a major risk and why the external aspects of security cannot be neglected.

The European security strategy

In 2003, the heads of state and governments of the European Union decided upon a security strategy of the European Union, which had been formulated by Javier Solana. Since then, this strategy has been updated (in 2008).

This European security strategy was in a way an answer to the security strategy of the Bush administration, which was based on the idea of coalitions of the willing. The European strategy promotes an effective multilateral system based on the Charter of the United Nations, and holds that no single country is able to tackle today's complex problems on its own.

At the time, the debate focused on the question of whether pre-emptive strikes could be justified under certain conditions. The European Council finally agreed on the statement that in an era of globalisation, distant threats may be as much a concern as those close to home and that the first line of defence will often be abroad.[2]

This statement is not only important for the external policy of the European Union but also for the further development of the Area of Freedom Security and Justice of the European Union as foreseen in the Stockholm Programme.

---

[2] European Council, *A secure Europe in a Better World, European Security Strategy*, presented by Javier Solana, Brussels, 12 December 2003.

Instruments of the European Union

Security is not an exclusive task of the armed forces and the police. Diplomacy, prevention, post-conflict reconstruction, development and dialogue are important elements of the security policy of the European Union.

The European Union disposes of a large number of instruments for maintaining peace and security. First and foremost is the External Action Service, which is at present being developed under the Treaty of Lisbon. This service will have to integrate the instruments for running civilian and military missions and to coordinate the security aspects of our neighbourhood and development policy.

In addition, debates in the European Parliament have demonstrated that there is a close connection between security and development. Poverty and bad governance are breeding grounds for crime and terrorism, and a secure environment is a *conditio sine qua non* for any economic and social development.

What recommendations for the future?

The implementation of the Treaty of Lisbon should be the occasion to improve the coordination of the different instruments that are at the disposal of the European Union. The External Action Service must be able to coordinate civilian and military missions of the European Union. The present instruments of analysis and planning have to be improved.

The common protection of our 'e-borders' should be strengthened. We need common standards for the equipment necessary for border surveillance. The role of Frontex, the European Agency for the Management of Operational Cooperation at the External Borders, should also be enhanced.

For mitigating natural and manmade disasters, we should implement the proposal for a civilian intervention force as proposed by Michel Barnier. This proposal was taken up in February 2010 by the European Parliament on the basis of the report of Arnaud Danjean. Such a force would be a major improvement to our capabilities of humanitarian intervention.

CONTRIBUTORS

Jacques Barrot is a member of the Constitutional Council of France. He was a Vice-President of the European Commission (2004–10), in charge of the Directorate-General for Justice, Freedom and Security from May 2008. Earlier, he held various parliamentary offices with different ministerial responsibilities in France, namely as Minister of Labour, Social Dialogue and Participation (1995), Minister of Health and Social Security (1979–81) and Minister of Commerce (1978–79).

Joaquín Bayo Delgado is a judge at the Barcelona Court of Appeal. From 2004 to 2009, he was European Data Protection Assistant Supervisor. Previously, he was Chief Judge of the Bench of Barcelona and a member of the Governing Chamber of the Superior Court of Catalonia, as well as a member of the ICT Commission of the General Council of the Spanish judiciary. Since 1989, he has acted as an expert for the Council of Europe on legal and judicial matters.

Emilio De Capitani is the Head of Unit responsible for the Secretariat of the European Parliament's Committee on Civil Liberties, Justice and Home Affairs. He joined the General Secretariat of the European Parliament in 1985, and has since held different management positions.

Madeline V. Garlick is the Head of the Policy and Legal Support Unit at the Bureau for Europe of the United Nations High Commissioner for Refugees (UNHCR). From 2004 to July 2009, she was Head of the EU Policy Unit at UNHCR's Liaison Office to the European Union.

Peter Hobbing is a Senior Associate Research Fellow at the Centre for European Policy Studies (CEPS) and a former official of the European Commission. After acquiring practical experience in border control/management at various German borders in the early 1980s, he served as an EU official in the fields of customs investigation, border control and anti-drugs cooperation. He held management positions at the European Commission's Directorate-General for Justice, Freedom and Security (1983–2001), in particular in the field of EU-wide enforcement cooperation. In 1999, he was an assistant to Adrian Fortescue, the first Director-General of this newly created body.

Kristine Kruma is a lecturer at the Riga Graduate School of Law and a doctoral student at Lund University. Since 2007, she has been a judge at the Constitutional Court of Latvia. She is also a member of the Odysseus Network, an academic network for legal studies on immigration and asylum in Europe. Her major research interests are the law of international organisations, citizenship, migration and integration.

Hasso Lieber is Secretary of State at the Ministry of Justice of the State of Berlin. Earlier, he served as Minister of the Interior of the State of Brandenburg (1992–99), as a delegate to the state parliaments of North Rhine-Westphalia and Brandenburg (1988–92), and as a judge at the District and Regional Courts of Bochum and the Higher Regional Court of Hamm.

Hans G. Nilsson is the Head of the Division on Judicial Cooperation at the Council of the European Union. During the Swedish presidency (July–December 2009), he joined the Permanent Representation of Sweden to the European Union as Minister and Head of the Justice and Home Affairs Counsellors. In this capacity, he was responsible for the negotiation of the Stockholm Programme on behalf of the Swedish presidency, and for aspects of the implementation of the Lisbon Treaty.

Johannes Vos served as an official at the Secretariat of the Council of the European Union from 1977 to 2008. He was in charge of justice and home affairs, especially matters concerning police cooperation, drugs and terrorism from 1986. Since January 2010, he has acted as an adviser on justice, liberty and security to the incoming Hungarian presidency.

Karl von Wogau is the Secretary-General of the European Security Foundation and President of the European Security Conference. Prior to that he was a member of the European Parliament (1979–2009), where he served as Chairman of the Subcommittee on Security and Defence (2004–09), as a member of the Special Committee on the access to sensitive information on European security and defence issues (2004–09), and as Chairman of the Committee on Monetary Affairs and Industrial Policy (1994–99).

Editors

Sergio Carrera is Research Fellow and Head of the Justice and Home Affairs Section at the Centre for European Policy Studies (CEPS). He is also a visiting lecturer at the University of Kent in Brussels, and an external expert on immigration and integration for the European Economic and Social Committee and the Committee of the Regions.

Alejandro Eggenschwiler is a Research Assistant at the Justice and Home Affairs Section at the Centre for European Policy Studies (CEPS).

Elspeth Guild is Jean Monnet Professor of European Migration Law at the Radboud University of Nijmegen. She is also a Senior Research Fellow at the Centre for European Policy Studies (CEPS) and a partner at the London law firm Kingsley Napley. She is a visiting professor at the London School of Economics (LSE) and teaches at the Department of War Studies at King's College London. She has acted as Special Adviser to the House of Lords and is a member of the European Commission's expert group on the policy needs for data on crime and criminal justice.

APPENDIX I. SELECTED LIST OF CEPS PUBLICATIONS ON JUSTICE AND HOME AFFAIRS (2002-10)

Books (CEPS and externally published)

Apap, J. (ed.) (2004), *Justice and Home Affairs in the EU: Liberty and Security Issues after Enlargement*, Cheltenham: Edward Elgar Publishing.

Apap, J. and M. Anderson (2002), *Striking a Balance between Freedom, Security and Justice in an Enlarged European Union*, CEPS, Brussels.

Balzacq, T. and S. Carrera (2005), *Migration, Borders and Asylum: Trends and Vulnerabilities in EU Policy*, CEPS, Brussels.

Balzacq, T. and S. Carrera (eds) (2006), *Security versus Freedom: A Challenge for Europe's Future*, Farnham: Ashgate Publishing.

Bigo, D., Carrera, S., Guild, E. and R. Walker (eds) (2010), *Europe's 21st Century Challenge: Delivering Liberty*, Farnham: Ashgate Publishing, forthcoming.

Carrera, S. (2008), *Benchmarking Integration in the EU: Analyzing the Debate on Integration Indicators and Moving It Forward*, Bertelsmann Foundation, Gütersloh.

———— (2009), *In Search of the Perfect Citizen? The Intersection between Integration, Immigration and Nationality in the EU*, Immigration and Asylum Law Series, Leiden: Martinus Nijhoff Publishers.

Guild, E. (2009), *Security and Migration in the 21st Century*, Cambridge: Polity Press.

Guild, E. and F. Geyer (eds) (2008), *Security versus Justice: Police and Judicial Cooperation in the European Union*, Farnham: Ashgate Publishing.

Guild, E., K. Groenendijk and S. Carrera (eds) (2009), *Illiberal Liberal States: Immigration, Citizenship and Integration in the EU*, Farnham: Ashgate Publishing.

CEPS Working Documents

Apap J. and S. Carrera (2003), *Towards a Proactive Immigration Policy for the EU*, CEPS Working Document No. 198, December.

Apap, J. (2004), *Problems And Solutions For New Member States In Implementing The JHA Acquis*, CEPS Working Document No. 212, October.

———— (2004), *Towards Closer Relationships: Requirements for More Effective JHA Cooperation in an Enlarged EU*, CEPS Working Document No. 211, October.

Apap, J. and A. Tchorbadjiyska (2004), *What about the Neighbours? The Impact of Schengen along the EU's External Borders*, CEPS Working Document No. 210, October.

Apap, J. and S. Carrera (2003), *Progress and Obstacles in the Area of Justice and Home Affairs in an Enlarging Europe*, CEPS Working Document No. 194, June.

Balzacq, T. (2008), *The External Dimension of EU Justice and Home Affairs: Tools, Processes, Outcomes*, CEPS Working Document No. 303, September.

Balzacq, T., D. Bigo, S. Carrera and E. Guild (2006), *Security and the Two-Level Game: The Treaty of Prüm, the EU and the Management of Threats*, CEPS Working Document No. 234, January.

Bertozzi, S. (2007), *Integration: An ever closer challenge*, CEPS Working Document No. 258, February.

———— (2007), *Legal Immigration: Time for Europe to Play its Hand*, CEPS Working Document No. 257, February.

———— (2008), *Schengen: Achievements and Challenges in Managing an Area Encompassing 3.6 million Km^2*, CEPS Working Document No. 284, February.

Brouwer, E. (2008), *The Other Side of Moon – The Schengen Information System and Human Rights: A Task for National Courts*, CEPS Working Document No. 288, April.

———— (2009), *The EU Passenger Name Record System and Human Rights: Transferring Passenger Data or Passenger Freedom?*, CEPS Working Document No. 320, September.

Carrera, S. (2004), *What does Free Movement Mean in Theory and Practice in an Enlarged EU?*, CEPS Working Document No. 208, October.

Carrera, S. (2005), *'Integration' as a Process of Inclusion for Migrants? The Case of Long-Term Residents in the EU*, CEPS Working Document No. 219, March.

———— (2007), *Building a Common Policy on Labour Immigration: Towards a Comprehensive and Global Approach in the EU?*, CEPS Working Document No. 256, February.

———— (2007), *The EU Border Management Strategy: FRONTEX and the Challenges of Irregular Immigration in the Canary Islands*, CEPS Working Document No. 261, March.

Carrera, S. and M. Formisano (2005), *An EU Approach to Labour Migration: What is the Added Value and the Way Ahead?*, CEPS Working Document No. 232, October.

Carrera, S. and R. Hernàndez i Sagrera (2009), *The Externalisation of the EU's Labour Immigration Policy: Towards Mobility or Insecurity Partnerships?*, CEPS Working Document No. 321, October.

Geyer, F. (2007), *Fruit of the Poisonous Tree – Member States' Indirect Use of Extraordinary Renditions and the EU Counter-Terrorism Strategy*, CEPS Working Document No. 263, April.

Guild, E. and S. Carrera (2005), *No Constitutional Treaty? Implications for the Area of Freedom, Security and Justice*, CEPS Working Document No. 231, October.

Guild, E. S. Carrera and A. Faure Atger (2009), *Challenges and Prospects for the EU's Area of Freedom, Security and Justice: Recommendations to the European Commission for the Stockholm Programme*, CEPS Working Document No. 313, April.

Hobbing, P. (2005), *Integrated Border Management at the EU Level*, CEPS Working Document No. 227, August.

Trauner, F. (2007), *EU Justice and Home Affairs Strategy in the Western Balkans: Conflicting Objectives in the Pre-Accession Strategy*, CEPS Working Document No. 259, February.

Trauner, F. and I. Krause (2008), *EC Visa Facilitation and Readmission Agreements: Implementing a New Security Approach in the Neighbourhood*, CEPS Working Document No. 290, April.

Wichmann, N. (2007), *The Intersection between Justice and Home Affairs and the European Neighbourhood Policy: Taking Stock of the Logic, Objectives and Practices*, CEPS Working Document No. 275, September.

CEPS Policy Briefs

Apap, J. and S. Carrera (2003), *Maintaining Security within Borders: Towards a Permanent State of Emergency in the EU?*, CEPS Policy Brief No. 41, November.

Apap, J. and S. Carrera (2004), *The European Arrest Warrant: A Good Testing Ground for Mutual Recognition in the Enlarged EU?*, CEPS Policy Brief No. 46, February.

Balzacq, T. and S. Carrera (2005), *The EU's Fight against International Terrorism: Security Problems, Insecure Solutions*, CEPS Policy Brief No. 80, July.

Bigo, D., S. Carrera and E. Guild (2008), *What Future for the Area of Freedom, Security and Justice? Recommendations on EU Migration and Borders Policies in a Globalizing World*, CEPS Policy Brief No. 156, March.

Carrera, S. and E. Guild (2007), *An EU Framework on Sanctions against Employers of Irregular Immigrants: Some Reflections on the Scope, Features and Added Value*, CEPS Policy Brief No. 140, August.

———— (2008), *The French Presidency's European Pact on Immigration and Asylum: Intergovernmentalism vs Europeanisation? Security vs Rights?*, CEPS Policy Brief No. 170, September.

Carrera, S. and F. Geyer (2007), *Terrorism, Borders and Migration: The Commission's 2008 Policy Strategy in the Area of Freedom, Security and Justice*, CEPS Policy Brief No. 131, June.

———— (2007), *The Reform Treaty & Justice and Home Affairs – Implications for the Common Area of Freedom, Security and Justice*, CEPS Policy Brief No. 141, August.

Geyer, F. (2007), *The External Dimension of EU Citizenship: Arguing for Effective Protection of Citizens abroad*, CEPS Policy Brief No. 136, July.

Guild, E. (2007), *EU Policy on Labour Migration: A First Look at the Commission's Blue Card Initiative*, CEPS Policy Brief No. 145, November.

———— (2007), *Inquiry into the EU-US Passenger Name Record Agreement*, CEPS Policy Brief No. 125, March.

———— (2007), *Making the EU Citizens' Agenda Work*, CEPS Policy Brief No. 122, February.

———— (2007), *Merging Security from the Two Level Game: Inserting the Treaty of Prüm into EU Law?*, CEPS Policy Brief No. 124, March.

Guild, E. and E. Brouwer (2006), *The Political Life of Data: The ECJ Decision on the PNR Agreement between the EU and the US*, CEPS Policy Brief No. 109, July.

Guild, E. and S. Carrera (2009), *Towards the Next Phase of the EU's Area of Freedom, Security and Justice: The European Commission's Proposals for the Stockholm Programme*, CEPS Policy Brief No. 196, August.

Guild, E., K. Groenendijk and S. Carrera (2008), *Ten Recommendations on Freedom, Security and Justice for the European Parliament Elections*, CEPS Policy Brief No. 173, October.

Guild, E., S. Carrera and F. Geyer (2008), *The Commission's New Border Package: Does It Take Us One Step Closer to a 'Cyber Fortress Europe'?* CEPS Policy Brief No. 154, March.

Lieber, H. (2008), *Checks and Balances: Dividing the Directorate General for Justice, Freedom and Security in Two – An Interior and a Justice Branch*, CEPS Policy Brief No. 158, April.

Moiny, Y. (2005), *Protection of Personal Data and Citizens' Rights of Privacy in the Fight against the Financing of Terrorism*, CEPS Policy Brief No. 67, March.

CEPS Liberty and Security in Europe

Acosta Arcarazo, D. (2009), *Latin American Reactions to the Adoption of the Returns Directive*, November.

Carrera, S. and A. Wiesbrock (2009), *Civic Integration of Third-Country Nationals: Nationalism versus Europeanization in the Common EU Immigration Policy*, October.

———— (2010), *Whose Citizenship to Empower in the Area of Freedom, Security and Justice? The Act of Mobility and Litigation in the Enactment of European Citizenship*, May.

Carrera, S. and M. Merlino (2009), *Undocumented Immigrants and Rights in the EU: Addressing the Gap between Social Sciences Research and Policy-Making in the Stockholm Programme?*, December.

De Vries, K., R. Bellanova and P. de Hert (2010), *Proportionality Overrides Unlimited Surveillance*, May.

Guild, E. (2010), *EU Counter-Terrorism Action: A Fault Line between Law and Politics?*, April.

Jimeno-Bulnes, M. (2010), *Towards Common Standards on Rights of Suspected and Accused Persons in Criminal Proceedings in the EU?*, February.

Pawlak, P. (2009), *Made in the USA? The Influence of the US on the EU's Data Protection Regime*, November.

Other publications (project series and special reports)

CHALLENGE

Bellanova, R. (2009), *A Model "Prêt-à-Exporter"? The 2008 German-US Agreement on Data Exchange*, CHALLENGE Research Paper No. 13, CEPS, Brussels, March.

Bigo, D., S. Carrera and E. Guild (2009), *The CHALLENGE Project: Final Policy Recommendations on the Changing Landscape of European Liberty and Security*, CHALLENGE Research Paper No. 16, CEPS, Brussels, September.

Bigo, D., S. Carrera, E. Guild and R.B.J. Walker (2007), *The Changing Landscape of European Liberty and Security: Mid-Term Report on the Results of the CHALLENGE Project*, CHALLENGE Research Paper No. 4, CEPS, Brussels, February.

Carrera, S. (2006), *A Comparison of Integration Programmes in the EU: Trends and Weaknesses*, CHALLENGE Papers No. 1, CEPS, Brussels, March.

Carrera, S. (ed.), J. Apap, L.F.M. Besselink, G.-R.de Groot, K. Groenendijk, E. Guild, J. Niessen and S. Pratt (2006), *The Nexus between Immigration, Integration and Citizenship in the EU*, CHALLENGE Collective Conference Volume, CEPS, Brussels, April.

Cesari, J. (2009), *The Securitisation of Islam in Europe*, CHALLENGE Research Paper No. 15, CEPS, Brussels, April.

Faure Atger, A. (2008), *The Abolition of Internal Border Checks in an Enlarged Schengen Area: Freedom of Movement or a Scattered Web of Security Checks?*, CHALLENGE Research Paper No. 8, CEPS, Brussels, March.

Geyer, F. (2008), *Taking Stock: Databases and Systems of Information Exchange in the Area of Freedom, Security and Justice*, CHALLENGE Research Paper No. 9, CEPS, Brussels, May.

Guild, E., S. Carrera and T. Balzacq (2008), *The Changing Dynamics of Security in an Enlarged European Union*, CHALLENGE Research Paper No. 12, October 2008.

Jeandesboz, J. (2008), *Reinforcing the Surveillance of EU Borders: The Future Development of FRONTEX and EUROSUR*, CHALLENGE Research Paper No. 11, CEPS, Brussels, August.

Jorry, H. (2007), *Construction of a European Institutional Model for Managing Operational Cooperation at the EU's External Borders: Is the FRONTEX Agency a Decisive Step Forward?*, CHALLENGE Research Paper No. 6, CEPS, Brussels, March.

Lodge, J. (2006), *Communicating (in)Security: A Failure of Public Diplomacy?*, CHALLENGE Research Paper No. 3, CEPS, Brussels, November.

Merlino, M. (2009), *The Italian (In)Security Package: Security vs. Rule of Law and Fundamental Rights in the EU*, CHALLENGE Research Paper No. 14, CEPS, Brussels, March.

Scandamis, N., F. Sigalas and S. Stratakis (2007), *Rival Freedoms in Terms of Security: The Case of Data Protection and the Criterion of Connexity*, CHALLENGE Research Paper No. 7, CEPS, Brussels, December.

Tsoukala, A. (2007), *Security Policies & Human Rights in Football Stadia*, CHALLENGE Research Paper No. 5, CEPS, Brussels, March.

Wessels, W. and F. Bopp (2008), *The Institutional Architecture of CFSP after the Lisbon Treaty: Constitutional Breakthrough or Challenges ahead?*, CHALLENGE Research Paper No. 10, CEPS, Brussels, June.

CEPS Special Reports

Aagaard, L. (2009), *A Shared Struggle for Truth and Accountability: Canada, Europe and Investigations into the Detention and Abuse of Citizens abroad*, CEPS Special Report, March.

Alegre, S. (2008), *The EU's External Cooperation in Criminal Justice and Counter-Terrorism: An Assessment of the Human Rights Implications with a Particular Focus on Cooperation with Canada*, CEPS Special Report, September.

Alegre, S., I. Ivanova and D. Denis-Smith (2009), *Safeguarding the Rule of Law in an Enlarged EU: The Cases of Bulgaria and Romania*, CEPS Special Report, April.

Carrera, S. and A. Faure-Atger (2009), *The Implementation of the of Directive 2004/38 in the Context of EU Enlargement: A Proliferation of Different Forms of Citizenship?*, CEPS Special Report, April.

Carrera, S. and F. Geyer (2009), *EU Policy on Education: The Impact on the Social Inclusion of the Vulnerable Groups*, CEPS Special Report, September.

Carrera, S. and M. Merlino (2009), *State of the Art on the European Court of Justice and Enacting Citizenship*, CEPS Special Report, April.

Faure Atger, A. (2009), *Education and Political Participation of Migrants and Ethnic Minorities in the EU: An Overview of the Literature*, CEPS Special Report, September.

Geyer, F. (2009), *The Educational System in Belgium*, CEPS Special Report, September.

——— (2009), *The Educational System in Luxembourg*, CEPS Special Report, September.

Guittet, E.-P. (2008), *Miscarriages of Justice and Exceptional Procedures in the 'War against Terrorism'*, Special CEPS Report, September.

Hobbing, P. (2008), *Tracing Terrorists: The EU-Canada Agreement in PNR Matters*, CEPS Special Report, September.

Macklin, A. (2009), *The Canadian Security Certificate Regime*, CEPS Special Report, March.

——— (2009), *Transjudicial Conversations about Security and Human Rights*, CEPS Special Report, March.

Mégie, A. (2009), *Replacing and Displacing the Law: The Europeanisation of Judicial Power*, CEPS Special Report, March.

Scherrer, A. (2009), *Good Practices as International Norms? The Modalities of the Global Fight against Organised Crime and Terrorism*, CEPS Special Report, March.

Tsoukala, A. (2008), *Security, Risk and Human Rights: A Vanishing Relationship?*, CEPS Special Report, September.

Other publications

Guild, E., S. Carrera and A. Eggenschwiler (2009), *Informing the Asylum Debate*, CEPS Background Briefing - In Preparation for the European Parliament Elections, May.

——— (2009), *Informing the Borders Debate*, CEPS Background Briefing - In Preparation for the European Parliament Elections, May.

——— (2009), *Informing the Data Protection Debate*, CEPS Background Briefing - In Preparation for the European Parliament Elections, May.

——— (2009), *Informing the Immigration Debate*, CEPS Background Briefing - In Preparation for the European Parliament Elections, May.